Mark Zupo

MIND YOUR BUSINESS!
The Secrets to Profiting From Your Life Experience!

The Ultimate Guide to Repurpose Your Life Experience, Passions, Education and Knowledge

By

Mark Zupo

"Make your life your business and Make your business your life!"

Mark Zupo

MIND YOUR BUSINESS!

The Secrets to Profiting From Your Life Experience!

Copyright © 2010 Mark Zupo. Mark Zupo International, LLC. All Rights Reserved in all media. No part of this book may be used or reproduced in any form without the prior written permission of the author and publisher. Printed in the United States of America.
© 2010 Mark Zupo International, LLC
All Rights Reserved in All Media

ISBN-10 0983994501

ISBN-13 9780983994503

Also available in audio / CD / eBook / Kindle™ formats

To order, contact: 1-678-640-0585
www.MarkZupo.com

Slippery Rock Press Publishing™
www.slipperyrockpress.com

Mark Zupo

DEDICATION

Dedicated to my wife,
Kay Stonesifer Zupo (1943-2005),
Without whose memory,
Love, strength, support and cheerful heart I would
be lost forever.

And to my Mother, Ann Rohrich, my Daughter, Traci, brother and sister, Chris Zupo and Rene Morasco for their undying support and love over the years.

I am forever grateful to you all.

And to my wife, Kathy Rule Zupo, a tower of strength, patience and support, who believed in me when others failed me.

In your trust.

CONTENTS

	Acknowledgments	i
1	Run Your Life like a Fortune 500 Company	10
2	Your Life is Big Business	30
3	Earn income from the work you love	38
4	Branding your life	44
5	Building your life product	78
6	Marketing your life	94
7	Building a mentorship	102
8	Leaving a legacy	114
9	Selling your life story	120
10	Your personal "ATM"	128
11	Your call to action	134

Acknowledgments

Most importantly, the first person to thank is my Mother. Expressing my gratitude to her would take this entire book and encompass every emotion known to man, so I will just offer the most sincere thanks a son can offer:

> *"All that I am and all that I hope to be, I owe to my mother."*
> **-Abraham Lincoln**

I would like to acknowledge all of the entrepreneurially- motivated people in the world, especially those who acted on their gut instincts, their visions of opportunity and their sense of independence. I would like to acknowledge anyone who ever had a brilliant idea or moment of inspiration when he thought could change the world. Those are the people who, because of their efforts to achieve more and succeed when the odds are against them, motivate me to success.

Each individual may or may not be proud of the part they played in my life experiences that have contributed to who and what I am today. Some people were instrumental to my failures and some influential to my successes. Either way, I am better man for it.

I am especially thankful for those people who denied me, stopped me, held me back, crushed my enthusiasm, said no, didn't care, cheated me, refused me, snubbed me, were resentful of me, were indignant, slighted me, and challenged me. To them, thanks for nothing—and ***thanks for everything!***

- **Mark Zupo**

Mark Zupo

*"We have met the enemy...
and he is us"*

- Walt Kelly

"Own your dreams and plan your success."
Mark Zupo - 2010

ABOUT THE AUTHOR

Mark Zupo is an "Accomplished Entrepreneur" who has devoted his life to helping others succeed in their goals and dreams. His goal is to help you fulfill your career goals and achieve financial freedom and independence by building the successful..."Business of You!". Mark's consulting and e-Business acumen remains unequaled as an <u>Life-Success Authority</u>. Mark is a leader, entrepreneur and mentor to many.

Mark Zupo is a dynamic and insightful speaker, recognized for his empowering and motivational focus to your success. As a driven leader with a commanding presence, he motivates, inspires, energizes and empowers his audience.

Mark Zupo has been the driving force in changing the lives of anyone within range of his voice. Mark's "3-Foot Rule" makes him one of the most sought-after speakers in his industry.

Mark's speaking career in industry spans 25 years and he has delivered more-than, 1,200 presentations. From his experiences he has authored and co-authored many books on self-development, business development techniques and marketing enterprises.

Mark Zupo

Introduction

Chances are you have spent life-time learning, studying, teaching and delivering information based on your experiences and expertise. Why haven't you profited from these passions while others have? If you're not sure of the steps necessary to find success in your passions, Mind Your Business will teach you. This book has been designed for those who want to change the direction of their lives and find success in their confidence, skills, background and passions. It is no secret that people have talent and experience, background and expertise. They have energy and enthusiasm that until now has been devoted to making someone else rich. They have visions of their success but don't know how to take advantage of, benefit from and profit from - until now. This book provides you the opportunity to profit from what you have learned and experienced.

This book, *Mind Your Business*, is for those who want to change the direction of their lives and find success in their confidence, skills, background and passions.

Are you one of the aforementioned people? Have you spent lifetime learning, experiencing and believing you can be the very best at who you are and what you do?

I have always believed that your destiny is determined by your decisions. Ultimately, the path your life takes is directly proportional to the amount of education you have and the amount of labor you put into it. Some of the guidance you get is a direct link to your past experiences.

In this book, *Mind Your Business*, you'll find the advice you need to form the business of "YOU!" You will find methods to help you grow as a business and profit from your expertise. This book will help you use your life's experience and passions to help other people do the same, while you earn a respectable fee for your services. After all, isn't that what a consultant does? He uses his knowledge to sell something.

How Can *Mind Your Business* Help You Succeed?

Most people have a set of rules they follow based upon their experiences, education, wants, needs and desires. When you choose to follow a path you question, you usually come to an end that is predictable and distasteful; so follow the leadership of those who have succeeded before you by using their experiences, failures and successes as a guide for your opportunities. After all, we want to emulate someone we respect and admire, and most of us are willing to change our lives to accommodate that desire.

We want to emulate those we respect and admire, and many of us are willing to change our lives to do so. With this in mind, I implore you to consider the following questions.

√ What is one thing you would change about your life?

This question comes with the hope that when you adopt a change, you will be better off. It is laced with the indication that when change is adopted, you will have a better life: fame, fortune, admiration. You will be brought to the forefront of others' attention.

You should be warned, though, that change also comes with risk, undefined hazards and ambiguous results. You will not be aware whether the risk is worth the reward until after you make the change, at which time it may be too late to reverse your decision.

This is like going back in time and changing whatever decisions may have been made along the way, thereby forever changing history. To the point of that scenario, your decisions and your motivation for success, freedom and wealth must be genuine and natural so you don't upset the balance of YOUR history.

√ What is stopping you from making that change?

Usually, we are held to our life's history by our decisions and opportunity. Notice I didn't say luck. I believe luck is the product of intuition, cognition, action and opportunity. I don't believe it is just happenstance. With that in mind, we have the ability to determine our course by some simple rules of intention. We must:

- Achieve What You Believe because You Believe You Can Achieve.
- Know thyself and Thy business because You Are Your Business.
- Build a Legacy: It is Inheritable.
- Find the Message that Helps YOU Help Other People.

The power of intention is the driving force that determines your fate as a leader, an entrepreneur and a success in any endeavor in your life.

√ What do I know that will make me a living?

The most valuable resource you have is what you know! You have spent your lifetime gaining wisdom and knowledge that others have used for their benefit. Until now, you have made others rich; you have supported their successes by giving away valuable information you have accumulated. We both know you have a passion someone else would pay for. What you may not know is that your passions, your experiences, your education and your training have provided you knowledge so valuable that you could spend your entire life in luxury. You simply need to sell some portion of it to others who need that information. All you need is a way to present this knowledge to them! This is what I will teach you.

"You sometimes have to set unrealistic goals to achieve realistic results!"
Mark Zupo – 2009

About Mind Your Business

This book is about know-how. Specifically, it is about your know-how. It is about the know-how you have spent a lifetime building while making mistakes, educating yourself to be the best you could be and experiencing all that life offers.

This book is about earning income from the work you love and the passions you have. It is about finding your personal place in the world; it is about using what you know and making a profit from it.

The idea for this book was drafted using a pen that I borrowed from a young lady who sat next to me on a flight from Los Angeles to Atlanta. Ashley S. and her husband Chris were returning from a vacation in Los Angeles, California, and didn't know who they were sitting next to or how it might change their lives. Although she did not know me, Ashley was kind enough to come to my aid; she lent me her pen to make notes for this book.

While talking to Ashley and her husband, I was overwhelmed by their commitment to each other and by Ashley's commitment to her business. Later, I couldn't help but reflect on how passionate Ashley was about her business, a business based on her own experiences, expertise and what she could do to help other people.

That is when it came to me - while sitting in the airplane next to this bright, young couple. That is when I figured out that the value of a business isn't as much about the value of service as it is about the value of service you provide. It is about you.

As luck would have it, my best ideas generally come to me when I am least prepared. I do my best when I am captive to myself in a situation that doesn't allow me to escape myself, such as when I am traveling on an airplane. I think well when I'm trapped in my truck, a Ford 150 pick-up, or when I'm trapped on an airplane, generally one that I am not flying.

I've always thought that my life is worth more than the life insurance that I carry. In fact, I believe in my heart that my life is worth more than all the gold in Fort Knox because my life is and will be as self-sustaining and as everlasting as I can make it. As long as my children continue to remember me, they will have the ability to capitalize on my life, just as Elvis's family has earned more on his fame than he ever did while he was alive.

I know that I am worth much more than anyone in corporate America is willing to pay me.

That, my friends, is unacceptable. It is unacceptable for me, and it is unacceptable for you.

Your attitude about your self-worth is directly related to your income, and your perceived self-worth will fluctuate in parallel as your income wavers or teeters in either direction. Additionally, what you learned in school has had the greatest effect on what you believe your self-worth to be. This has been a great disservice to every American.

A true entrepreneur will find solutions where seemingly none exist, and he or she will triumph, no matter the risks or challenges. When we become educated to the value of what we desire, as opposed to the cost of the same, we can remove the blinders that keep us from success. In this book, you will find motivation, inspiration and guidance.

Take what you learn from this book and run with it, preferably to the bank. You will learn from experts who have built iconic lives out of a simple idea, a simple marketing plan and some luck and guts. Everyone has enough life experience to make a fortune, although most aren't aware of the power of their life experiences. You will discover that one's value is never as much as his worth until he learns how to market his life experience to the masses.

Chapter 1

Run Your Life like a Fortune 500 Company

As a young man, I was always blessed by the belief that I deserved to be rich. It wasn't arrogance or elitism. I thought I was just as good as anybody else and that I could achieve anything that anyone else did if I worked hard enough. It took me many years of struggle to learn that hard work is not the answer; smart work is.

Having struggled throughout my life through trial and error in many business ventures, I've been fortunate enough to learn a few key insights that ultimately lead me to success and accomplishment. It wasn't until I really understood the concept of choice that my reasons to be "rich" came to me.

That is why I decided to evaluate my understanding for wanting riches.

They are what I call "To's":

- The **need** to
- The **want** to
- The **have** to
- The **choice** to
- The **love** to

And finally...

- The *call* to

The Choices We Make

I believe the foundation for any desire is the choices we make, which is a result of our intentions. Wanting to be rich is more complicated than simply having a desire to achieve wealth. Having wealth does not guarantee happiness, and happiness does not guarantee wealth. Being rich is more a state of mind than a state of economics.

Based on personal experience, my evaluation of the need to be rich, I believe the following categories of intention are crucial to success.

- **Need To   =   Survival**

The need for wealth comes from a need to

survive and to provide for the continued survival of your family. Without some money, you will certainly increase your opportunities for a shorter life. This comes from a lack of medical attention, of shelter from the elements and of food to sustain your health.

- **Have To = Security**

When you think you must have a lot of money to be secure, it is an indication that you are insecure in your strengths and abilities to survive in the comfortable manner to which you have become accustomed.

- **Want To = Social Gain**

The desire to be rich is a self-seeking desire that gives you recognition among your peers, superiors and subordinates, as well as in the social community.

- **Choice To = Self Growth and Development**

One must make a conscious choice to pursue the avenue that might ultimately lead to success and riches. Choice usually translates to action, and action gets results.

- **Love To =   Self Fulfillment**

Having great regard for the things you've

acquired throughout your life reveals a humble appreciation for their value beyond their simple worth based upon price. A love to have riches indicates more of your appreciation for what wealth can do for others than what it can do for your self-fulfillment.

- **Called To = Inspiration**

I often have said, "I was called to be rich." I firmly believe that you deserve to be rich and that having access to riches is a right rather than a privilege. A calling ignites your efforts to pursue the path that leads you to the goal you focus on. Your calling, your inspiration, is your motivation.

Each of these attributes of intention amounts to your accountability as an achiever. How you are ultimately held accountable can be good or bad, depending on how you govern your intentions, actions and choices. Whatever intention has initially directed you to success or failure can be modified to make the outcome meet your desires.

> *"Make your business your life and...*
> *Make your life your business"*
> *- Mark Zupo*

I grew up on a farm in Pennsylvania doing my chores and taking care of my responsibilities because I was a responsible young man. I **need**ed to complete my chores to get what I wanted to eat and to survive. I **had** to complete my chores to insure that the farm continued to grow and prosper. I **want**ed to complete my chores because I loved what I did and would ultimately get punished if I didn't!

I **chose** to complete my chores because it felt good to have some control. I **love**d to complete my chores because it was what my life was all about: helping others to grow. I was **call**ed to complete my chores because it was what gave my life meaning.

The responsibility I learned from growing up on a farm taught me many things. It taught me that accountability was the end result of my actions, and if I didn't conduct myself responsibly, the accountability could be severe. Don't complete the chores you are assigned and you become accountable for your inactions. This has serious implications on a farm. As a young man under the rule of a demanding step-father, I felt more often than not that the punishment didn't fit the crime. I did learn, though, that we must be accountable for all we do.

"Failure is the major contributor to success."

Unknown

I could not have been more fortunate

than to have grown up with adult-like responsibilities. The lessons of farm life were many, intense and lasting. A young person learns many things about life when growing up on a farm, and he takes it to his adult life in the forms of character, temperament, ethics and respect.

It does not matter that I did not stay on the farm, as my step—father would have liked, and use these skills. I carried each of them forward to find my passions and rewards in other arenas. There were many lessons from my youth that have stayed with me throughout the course of my life, but three were the most valuable to me.

The First Lesson: Mindset

In this life of technology, impersonal modes of communication, corporate indoctrination and cultural diversity, a person can be overwhelmed with an identity crisis. Who am I? What do I do? Why do I do it? For whom am I doing it? What is my real value? What am I really worth...and to whom?

You can see that your mindset is as crucial as any other aspect of the process to define who you are and what you can contribute, especially what you can contribute that will make you money! These characteristics are borne from the duty of all men and women, and they become the lasting impression of who you are. They are also the business of your life. They are the business of your experiences that you can profit from if you know how.

- Adversity Builds Character.......and **experience**.
- Responsibility Builds Respect...and **confidence**.
- Accountability Builds Honor................and **ethics**.
- Privilege Builds Humility......................and **trust**.
- Dependability Builds Trust.........and **credibility**.

A number of people have passed through my life. Some did good things and some did not. I have great admiration and respect for those who touched my life in a positive way; I learned great lessons from them. One such person was my Uncle Ed. Uncle Ed was a big guy. It was obvious to me that he had strength and power, but he was as gentle as a lamb. It didn't matter when I had an opportunity to speak to him, whether it was casually, by design or just because I was wasting time, I learned a great deal from everything he had to say.

Ok...I know now that he was talking to a kid and that he tempered his comments to fit my age, but it didn't matter because the insight, motivation and lessons he gave were just as valuable then as they are today.

-You deserve to be Rich!

My Uncle Ed was a kind and good man whose gentle ways were often mistaken for weakness. On the contrary, Uncle Ed was a strong and dutiful man with a great power of influence and with an enviably dynamic vision.

Once, I had the opportunity to stay with him for a few weeks, which gave me many opportunities to talk to him "man to man." Having the foresight of a dreamer and achiever-to-be, I asked him, "What will the future bring for me? Will I be rich?" He answered as only Uncle Ed could answer, **"Markey-Boy, you deserve to be rich!"**

That was all I needed to hear. It was the license I needed to achieve my goals of wealth and freedom. I was able to visualize my future right there and then. The best thing about that vision is that I saw I would earn a living from doing the things I love, instead of from working for someone else as I helped to make him or her rich. It didn't take college to teach me that; it just took working the farm.

-The more I have...the happier I'll be

When you grow up on a real working farm, you have little and you have much. When you try to calculate the value of your material items, it appears you have very little. When you perceive what you have in the sense of opportunity, life experience and blessing, it adds up to unbelievable fortune.

One misconception that I had while growing up on the farm was that "If I had more I would be happier." Not so. I learned this only after amassing a fortune for the second time in my life and losing it all - again. After losing a million dollar fortune for the second time, I was actually somewhat relieved to be without all that money again. There was relief from the pressure of how to invest it, when to sell stocks, who might try to steal it and who would fight over it after I was gone.

Who would have ever thought that I would earn more than a million dollars in my life...let alone that I would do it twice? And who would ever have thought that I could lose it twice as well? As smart as I thought I was and as smart as other people thought I was, I failed to invest in my future properly to protect my legacy.

My future successes have been determined by my commitment to succeed. I have never lost that passion, and I live by its credo every day of my life.

"Commitment is what transforms a promise into reality."
Mark Zupo – 2007

-Future Achievement is a Poor Plan

Having amassed a fortune before I was thirty years old was, in itself, a banner achievement for a kid. At twenty-five, I was worth a million dollars. Actually, I was worth more than a million dollars...but who's counting?

Earning that kind of money seemed easy because the timing was right, the economics were right and, more importantly, no one told me that I couldn't do it!

My greatest success came when a man, who we will not name here for legal reasons as he went to prison for fraud and embezzlement, talked me into a real estate investment venture. As luck would have it, I came up with the money to invest; and I bought, on his suggestion, a share of a condominium.

Three days later, a mysterious fire claimed the condominium, which was located in a famous ski resort town. I collected the insurance money for my share of the appraised value of the condo, which equaled three times what I had invested. I made **forty-thousand dollars** on a **five thousand dollar** investment in a weekend! The investment was legal and I was hooked.

Knowing what to do with the money was mystifying. I seemed to have the skills to make money but lacked the skills to keep it for any length of time. The spoils of opportunity for me were also the curse of my accomplishments.

I learned how to spend like I was a millionaire simply because I was. I turned that money into other real estate investments that never seemed to lose money. Every investment I made turned out to be a gold mine. It seemed like I couldn't lose. What I didn't learn, however, was that I needed an education...a business education.

Over the next ten years I went on to buy condominiums, single family homes, townhouses, duplexes, strip malls and a food franchise. Thinking I was well off in my own right led me to think that I didn't need a college degree; I had earned my right as an entrepreneur by collecting money! I would be wrong again.

What I would have learned if I had attended college were lessons in running my life like a business, necessary lessons if I were to be the head of a household, to have a family and to provide for them a good life of less hardship and toil than I had experienced to this point. I failed to plan!

"Today's mess – tomorrow's success."
Mark Zupo - 2003

-Success Doesn't Bring Happiness...Happiness Brings Success

A valuable lesson I had to learn was what I call "The Lesson of the Wealthy." To be more specific, it was how to be wealthy, which in turn meant how to keep the wealth I made. This is valuable because I seemed happier when I had money than when I did not. No surprise there.

What I discovered was that it was my family who made me happy, not my money. Lose a child to a drunk driver, lose a wife to cancer, lose everything you have ever earned to the economy, and you learn hard lessons in humility, respect, dignity and...happiness.

-Baptism by Fire

"You can't have a message until you've had a mess.

You can't have a testimony until you've had a test."

- Unknown

I am not sure from where the term "Baptism by Fire" comes, but I assume it means that one's understanding is defined by the end result of an intense experience. This is how I gained some valuable insights into how I should reflect before I say what I'm thinking!

What the Nay-Sayers Say:

- Those who say, **"I wouldn't"** really mean, "I would if the circumstances were safer."

- Those who say, **"I shouldn't"** really mean, "I should when I feel more comfortable about my confidence."

- Those who say, **"I couldn't"** really mean, "I could if I were more secure in my decision-making and risk-taking abilities."

- Those who say anything less than **"I Will"** may never succeed without taking action!

When I say I wouldn't, shouldn't or couldn't, it is usually because I am fearful about proceeding to act. In fact, however, I never fail to act because I am less afraid of action than I am of what people will think of my failures.

The Second Lesson: Commitment

-Passion Delivers Purpose

There are three principles of absolute accomplishment: Vision, Focus and Action. These three principles are the foundation for achievement, regardless of one's intention, direction or motivation.

- **Vision = Success**

Any goal you have is a product of your vision- in the idea stage, in the formulation stage or in the development stage. Regardless, your vision keeps your focus on the results rather than on the path.

- **Focus = Direction**

Your focus to achieve the end result of your vision is the guide that leads you and keeps you on track. Your focus is your direction and the force that compels you to move forward without distraction.

- **Action = Results**

The action you take is the force that drives you to achievement at every level of your battle. Your action at any level delivers results at every level. If you maintain your vision, preserve your focus and take action, your success will never be diminished by a lack of results.

"Power with purpose, purpose with power."
Mark Zupo – 2010

Your vision, focus and action will

- **Change Lives**
- **Empower People**
- **Lead People**
- **Create Independence**
- **Turn Adversity into Triumph**

The Third Lesson:

5 Principles of Success

1. **Focus on the desired results.**

    Make a plan and follow it to the letter. Never give up. Always follow through with it, from the first detail to the last detail. Have ***PASSION!***

2. **Develop your situational awareness.**

    Learn to recognize problems and obstacles that will come up. Be ready for them. Have a plan of attack to fix them. Be aware of potential risks; accept that they exist and are waiting for you to resolve them immediately. Have ***NO FEAR!***

3. **Increase mental flexibility.**

   The state of your mind is a state of mind! Control it, manage it, and use it to your advantage. Be sharp; educate yourself. Exercise your functional obedience to your plan, your vision and your focus. Have **_PERSISTANCE!_**

4. **Maintain mental excellence.**

   Develop a routine for stretching your mind and body to maintain sharpness and acute abilities. Exercise your mind and body regularly. No-one can make you a success but you! Have **_PERSPIRATION!_**

5. **Take action!**

   Remember, "Ignorance on fire always beats knowledge on ice!" Action...Action...Action. Those who start and finish what they start are the successful few. They are the winners, the champions, the conquerors, the victors and most importantly...the rich! Have **_PURPOSE!_**

-Make Your Business...YOUR BUSINESS!

Entrepreneurship is natural and instinctive. It is innate in every one of us. Entrepreneurship, from the earliest history of man, is a natural method of survival, which we use every day in some form or another. We sell ourselves to our boss and our friends; we sell ourselves to our spouse, our peers, and our clients. We desire to be admired every day. Turning that into income is easier than you think. We simply have to channel that desire for admiration into an income-producing vehicle.

When we attach capitalism to entrepreneurship, we get income from our efforts. We can get paid to be who we are by people who admire who we are for what we do or for what we have accomplished. This isn't being arrogant or conceited, but rather it is using our talents to capitalize on our strengths and accomplishments.

Have you ever read an autobiography? Have you ever purchased a book or audio-CD from someone who has done something that you would like to do?

> **"Once the mind of man is expanded to the dimensions of new thought, it never retracts to its original size or shape."**
> **Oliver Wendell Holmes, Jr.**

Taking advantage of our ability to convey what we know into a product is what we want to achieve. It is **The Business of YOU™**. The business of you results in the freedom, success and profit you want. Understanding the net value of money delivers the freedom that is your ultimate goal. When you understand this concept, you are well on your way to achieving the success.

If you know what you want, if you know how to get what you want and if you know what you would do to get it, then you have the tools that will lead you to act on your vision and achieve your goals.

The NET Value of money:

- Gets you what you want.
- Drives you to success.
- Forms desire to acquire it.
- Determines what you would do to get it.
- Establishes what you can do for other people too!

Later in this book, we'll discuss how you will take what you have learned throughout your life and turn it into a product that you can rely on forever. The reason this will work: it is all about you.

Who better than you to capitalize on what you have spent your lifetime learning? Now is the time to use what

you have learned for your benefit.

There are a few methods that will help you skyrocket your visibility and recognition as an authority or an expert in your field or your niche. Once you have seen the process, you'll be well on your way to changing your life!

Free Enterprise + Entrepreneurship + Knowledge = Freedom

"Your actions at any level deliver results at every level."

Mark Zupo – 2010

Chapter 2

Your Life is Big Business and... No One Taught You How To Run It!

The founding idea for this book was the realization that our lives amount to big business if we are taught how to manage, market and capitalize on them. Having worked to make other people rich was a lesson in managing them, marketing them and inspiring them to capitalize on their abilities, virtues and abilities.

Every successful person, male or female, has many of the same traits. These people are usually entrepreneurial by design. They are driven by their need to accomplish results of some sort, and they are only satisfied by achievements from their own efforts. These people are driven to achieve levels of success that are just as possible for any average person as they are for the high achievers. Everyone is divided into three groups. There are those who make things happen, those who watch things happen, and those who wonder what happened. Only one of these groups ever finds riches, happiness, success, or achievement.

In *Mind Your Business*, you will find a simple means of taking the focus off your employer, your relatives or your friends. We need to accept that we control our lives, which then has a profound effect on our successes. When you begin to look at yourself as a product, you can visualize putting your expertise and experience into a sellable format that others will buy to learn how to do the same for themselves.

> *"The bigger your mess...*
> *the bigger your message."*
> **John F. Kennedy**

As children we need the permission to do anything, as adults we need the purpose to do anything and as entrepreneurs we need the opportunity to do anything. The focus of this example is to highlight that it us up to us. Only we can do what is best for us if we do it by design.

Developing Your Credibility

- **Standing Out**

    -Passion, Power, Persistence, Purpose

People function differently. Remember the three groups:

- Those who **make** things happen.
- Those who **watch** things happen.
- Those who **wonder** what happened.

Which are you? This is the time for honesty. Giving yourself more credit than you deserve is only fooling you. If you don't like what you hear in your answer, now is the time to change it. It isn't necessary to be too hard on yourself; just be honest.

Your purpose - What's in Your Plan?

"Build your strengths by nailing down your weaknesses."
Mark Zupo – 2009

Desperation

If you are seeking fame, fortune, success and affluence out of a sense of desperation, any plan will ultimately fail. That's because desperate people make decisions in haste to try to achieve, as quickly as possible, the outcome they desire. This will never do.

Determination

When we are determined to make a quick decision, it usually is at the expense of critical thinking and decisive planning. Thoughtless determination never translates into an effective plan. This type of determination typically causes us to make a do-or-die decision or to perform an irreversible action due to a need to have accomplished something at any cost.

Dedication

Although dedication is an admirable trait, it is also a condition that lends to staying the course, when a better decision may be folding the cards and moving on to another option. We have options. We should use every resource at our disposal to weigh every decision and then to arrive at the correct decision, as opposed to the quick decision.

Inspiration

Inspiration, when making decisions and planning actions, is a valuable tool as long as the outcome and goal are well defined. Having a specific goal is the key that inspiration will lead to innovation and ingenuity. Ingenuity has been the lifeblood of American advancement in technology and in the modernization of our society.

Perspiration

Another key resource and essential quality in the planning process is your personal effort. You should make use of the physical attributes of your *perspiration factor* when making life-changing and self-empowering decisions. Success is appreciated to a greater degree when sweat-equity is a contributing factor.

Motivation

A final contribution to your planning process, motivation is a fundamental ingredient to achieving any goal and to determining the outcome of your decisions. Motivation may be the greatest factor in the planning processes because it is the catalyst for every action toward a predetermined goal. Unless you are motivated, success may be just a dream.

Visibility, Credibility, Profitability

Three critical elements to your success are visibility, credibility and profitability. *Visibility* creates the awareness of you and what you are presenting to an audience of believers, followers or students. Establishing visibility can be an expensive and tedious process, but it can be a vehicle for absolute success. Some considerations of the utmost importance are

a. You are true to your followers, students or believers.

b. You provide valuable content to them.

c. You nurture their participation by your contribution to their success.

d. You remain available to them to educate them and to foster their agendas.

Once your visibility is created through social media or personal appearance, the attributes that appeal to a following are the groundwork for establishing your credibility. Your *credibility* will allow you to present your ideas, proposals and initiatives. Your ideas will be accepted because of the trust established from your previous offerings and from the security in your word as reliable.

Methods to establish your credibility:

This is an important step in the process of allowing people to see you as a trusted resource:

1. Perspective:

Visualize your success as if it has already happened.

2. Philosophy

Develop a winning attitude that never waivers.

3. Personal Path

Take action steps that deliver results.

4. Position

Establish your authority with leadership.

5. Popularity

Manage your presence with other industry leaders.

6. Partnerships

Deliver your message with similar quality partners.

7. Progress

Measure everything you do with your goal in mind.

8. Press

Advertise who you are! Promote, Promote, Promote.

9. Performance

Deliver more than is expected in quality, rather than in quantity.

10. Products

Sell what you know. Who can do that better than you can?

11. Passion

Have heart. It is the foundation of your success.

12. Pay

You have to teach people to give you money!

You have to -
teach people to give you money!

Profitability will be the final condition to ensure success. This may sound a bit contradictory; however, unless you are and remain profitable, you cannot continue to promote yourself and to present offerings in the future. Promotion is expensive and presentation costs time, which also translates to expense.

Visibility and credibility, under the right guidance and in the right conditions, can and usually do convert into profitability. Keep in mind that the business world is a dynamic and ever-changing beast. It must be tamed at every turn lest it overwhelm both you and your profit machine.

> **"Love your work and work what you love"**
>
> **Mark Zupo – 2007**

Chapter 3

Earning Income from the Work You Love

"A person's worth to society is measured by their wealth when in fact

their wealth should be measured by their worth to society."
- **Unknown**

It is a mistake to allow any corporation to determine your value based upon what they think you are worth. Your value is what they determine your importance is to them; your worth is what they determine your significance is to them. Believe me when I say that the two are nowhere close in definition.

-Your Value or Your Worth

What is of greater importance is what *you* determine your value and worth to be? If value is **importance** and worth is **significance**, then consider the beneficiaries of those attributes and which is of greater importance to them. What you represent to your beneficiaries will be determined long after you are gone. Your value to them is your importance as it relates to their needs. Your value to your employer, for example, is that you sit at your desk and do your job. Your worth, however, is determined by who you are and what you represent. Your worth is your significance; it is your character, your enthusiasm and what you bring to the lives of those around you.

If you are a person who works for a business that you love, then you are the product of your own success. The "business of you" is vastly more important to your loved ones and associates than is a business you represent for someone else.

Can your children say that the gold watch you received after working for someone else represents who you are, who you have been for 30 years or more? A gold watch is a poor replacement for a legacy; it can never represent your value. However, your legacy as an entrepreneur, innovator, mentor, philanthropist, guide, educator, parent or guardian is and can be your legacy; it can and does represent your worth.

-Worth vs. Value,

-Want vs. Need,

-Deserve vs. Expect.

When you consider your **worth** to society, to a family and to a civilization in general, you are making a determination of the merit of your existence as it relates to their benefit. Your worth is your importance and usefulness in the name of some purpose. Your worth to the world is incalculable because you are continually delivering some benefit as you grow and develop.

The **value** you provide is of some significance to someone or something. Value represents the highest of quantity and quality.

Want comes from a deficiency or lack of something, such as money, freedom, independence and control. Wanting means you are absent a desirable trait or talent.

Usually one wants more money or a better education, but do we actually need more money or a better education to use what we already have? Interestingly, in countries where people live in poverty, what we think of as the necessities of life are virtually unknown; in these countries, want is also unknown.

Need is a requirement. Circumstances usually determine the degree of need, the sense of urgency. Do you want to be rich or do you need to be rich? Money may be a need, but it may also be a want depending on what your intentions are, such as philanthropy. Does the bearer of great riches _need_ to give his money away or does the bearer _want_ to give his money away?

Deserve is to be worthy of, qualified for, or have a claim to reward based upon an action or certain qualities possessed. You may deserve success, based upon some remarkable effort in a competition. However, you may not realize the success because another person was dominant in the competition. Perhaps his scores or actions were superior to yours. The lesson here is that we may *deserve* to win, but we may not get what we *expect*.

Expect is our ability to anticipate and hope for the outcome we want, which is often to be a success either in a single venture or in multiple projects. We can hope we will be rich, we anticipate we will be rich and we await riches! Interestingly, most positive, successful people talk about what they *expect* when they describe their future successes. They have some justification, founded in logic and reasoning, for their expectations. They are justified in their expectations because with positivity and experience comes with the confidence that success is likely.

Sometimes favorable results are simply the products of expectations. I recall a story about the legendary boxer, Mohammed Ali.

When he was asked by reporter Howard Cosell why he thought he was "the greatest boxer of all time," he replied, "Because I said so!" Ali's confidence was rooted in his expectation of beating all of his rival boxers. He expected to be victorious, which bolstered his own confidence and ultimately corrupted his opponent's confidence.

"The obstacles to success are not the things we think we need to be successful; It's getting rid of the baggage we already have that get in the way of our success."

Mark Zupo - 2010

Chapter 4

Branding your Life

You're brand is your reputation and it encompasses the following:

- **Your personal reputation.**

- **Your unique promise of value.**

- **The permission to be yourself.**

Why did personal branding begin? Personal branding grew from a faster business world which is increasingly driven with technology and innovation. As well, a new niche of personal egos has been created from the increasing desire to be recognized for our unique strengths and contributions.

Branding is all about the image of a business. In this case, remember, the business is you. This image should not only include style, emblems and logos, but it should also include the image of quality. The image perceived should be one of total quality and reliability.

From this point on, when we discuss a brand and a reputation, we will refer to you as the business and, respectively, the business as you.

When we think of certain political figures, movie stars or television personalities, we usually recognize them by their names: Oprah, Madonna, Sting, Sarah Palin, Rosie, Chevy Chase, Donald Trump, Connie Chung, George Clooney, Ice-T, Regis...etc. You recognize exactly what they represent when you hear their names.

Branding is about the individuals or the businesses and what makes them different from their competitors. The purpose of a brand is to distinguish you from your competition.

Once you have a distinguishing impact that establishes your personal brand, an advertising campaign can be much more effective. Branding includes many factors which help you be successful:

- **A website *"webinality,"***

- **Marketing efforts**

- **Anything that gives a company an identity**

Consumers, because there is a psychology in what motivates their purchasing decisions, wholeheartedly trust a corporate image. A small company with a brand, when it practices the right techniques, looks just as good as any large corporation who has spent millions of dollars to be recognized in their industry. Brands enhance your confidence as a business owner, and they build confidence in the consumer's mind. Branding indicates that you really can deliver what you promise.

Branding offers the perception of consistency. Inwardly, it gives direction to employees to deliver on established consumer expectations. Outwardly, a brand's consistency provides visibility that represents the professional appearance which will remain in the memory of a consumer.

One concept that consumers often attach to a brand is called brand equity. A brand is often considered to be an asset. For example, if you have developed a brand that is well known for being a top distributor of computers, your brand will be worth more than the brand of your competitor who is known to provide lesser-quality products.

Branding Basics

Branding is about the person or the business, and what makes *them* different y*ou*. Distinguishing yourself from others is a critical step in creating the "***Business of You***." I have created seminars and my Mind Your Business ™ training resources to teach you how to find your strengths and demonstrate your uniqueness to others, which will make you, stand out from your competitors.

Branding is all about shaping customers' perception of you or your company. Your brand is the promise that you make to customers. The ultimate goal is to spark an emotional connection and to create a positive feeling, resulting in customer loyalty to a specific product.

Most customers remain true to products they enjoy. It is very common for a customer to be impressed with a brand and continue to buy a product based upon that brand. Ultimately, you want to create these feelings of loyalty to bring the customers back for more. The benefits of personal branding are

- Self-understanding of what makes you valuable
- Visibility and presence to help achieve your goals

- Differentiation from your competition
- Wealth that comes from strong brand recognition.
- Continuity from resolve to success.

Your Mission and Vision

The mission and vision statement of your company should uphold excellence in providing a quality product to your customers. These are statements about your company regarding the ultimate goals you wish to achieve. Many companies focus their vision or mission on their employees, while others extend their mission outward to the customers. There should be a fine mix of both.

The vision and mission statements are very important for every business, no matter how big or small. As you craft your vision and mission statements, ensure your brand works well and that it matches what you say you want to deliver. You must also determine the benefits and features of your business and have a clear picture of their impact. You will need this information when you focus on developing your brand.

Many customers do not read vision or mission statements. However, that doesn't mean that you shouldn't take these statements seriously. Your vision and mission statements both are a part of the branding process because they define what your company is all about. These two statements need to be believed and practiced by all the employees and the staff of the company.

Benefits and Features of Your Products or Services

A big part of creating a brand for your business is showing customers why your products and services are the best to buy.

Differentiation occurs by proving the benefits of doing business with you to the consumers. Determine the benefits of what you are offering. Why do customers benefit when they shop with or buy from you? You will have a very hard time establishing a brand if you cannot determine the differentiating benefits of your products or services.

The specific features of your products and services are also important. Determine the specific features; which ones stand out from the rest or provide the biggest benefit? These may be a target for your marketing campaign.

Customers' Perception

Branding is about customer perception...and perception is everything! When you want to create a brand, you want to create a perception that you are the best, that you provide quality and that you deliver what you promise.

When you are building a branding campaign, it is important to have a good idea of what the customers currently think of you. Today, customers may not know you exist, or they may have a negative attitude toward your business because you haven't been delivering top-notch products or services. You might think customers absolutely love you, when they are really avoiding you or your products because of the poor quality of your product. Knowing what the customers think is very important. Creating a brand based upon customer input can be successful, especially if you change the design of something for the customers. This gives them a sense of ownership, and it shows them you really do care.

Audience

Audience is everything. If you do not know your audience, you cannot begin creating a brand for a product or a company.

There are many reasons that your target audience must be considered. Knowing your audience well will work for you over time.

The audience is the targeted customer base that you are hoping to reach. Audience considerations may include gender, age, geographical regions, and more. The age of an audience must be considered when branding. If you are targeting a younger and hipper crowd, they may want to see a brand that is vibrant and trendy.

If your audience is older and more sophisticated, they may be looking for a brand displaying more professionalism.

The gender of an audience is often an issue, especially if you are selling gender-specific items. However, when you create a brand for men, remember that you can create ad campaigns targeting women to purchase the products as gifts for men.

A customer's income isn't something that many businesses who are developing a brand think about when they consider their audience. This is often where companies go wrong. If you are selling a video gaming system for several hundred dollars in a local store, and the average income of families in the area is less than $25,000 a year, families may not be able to afford the product. You cannot sell an expensive product to a poor audience.

Also, people with a very high income may not consider purchasing a cheap product. The value of your brand must match the income of the people you think will be your primary target customers.

Know Your Audience

There are many things about your audience that you must know when you are creating a brand. If you do not have a clear understanding of your audience, you will fail. It is important to narrow down your target audience based on age, gender (only if specific), geographical region (only if specific) and income level. Once defined, you will know your specific audience, for example, 20- to 30-year-old, left-handed, male golfers.

Some brands may not be this specific. However, the more you can narrow down your audience, the more your brand will separate you from the competition. You will have fewer competitors with whom to compete.

Logos

Today it is common for people to say that a logo is everything when it comes to branding. This couldn't be further from the truth. A logo is important in many ways when branding; however, it is not where the rubber meets the road. A logo is one of the smallest forms of branding.

About Logos

It is common for companies not to have a graphical logo that represents their company.

They may just have the name of their business in bright, basic letters in front of the store. Many online site owners do the same and simply write the name of the website in bold letters at the top. Ever hear of IBM or AT&T?

A logo may be a creative way of writing your company name in bold or italic lettering, in a special font, or in different colors; it may even contain a picture. An iconic logo is the golden arches of McDonald's. This is a symbol that everyone recognizes. When approaching the arches on the side of the road, people immediately know the restaurant indicated.

Does a Logo Really Help You Sell?

There is a lot of hype about logo creation. The web is saturated with companies offering to design the perfect company logo. Logos do not help you sell products. They are not responsible for increasing revenues. No one buys a product because the logo is cool or professionally designed. They do, however, have value.

Logos create a positive impact for a business. A company with a logo versus a company that does not have a logo looks more professional and appears to be a more credible place to shop. This is because a professional logo creates an image. For example, employees wearing plain blue shirts in a store do not look as professional as employees wearing the same plain blue shirt with a company logo stamped on the top left chest area.

Logos are a part of the perception you create for your customers. Your goal in designing a logo is to create an image that has an emotional impact with the customers. This doesn't mean to add an emotional picture or throw in a tagline to make people cry.

Taglines, like logos, should have an impact; they should make a promise you are going to deliver. Pictures should not be in logos at all; however, if you choose to put one in a logo, ensure it is small and not too busy.

Building Trust and Recognition

Building and earning trust, which is also building recognition, can be a difficult task in the branding process. There are many ways that you build trust and recognition. However, you must start within the organization; within the organization you can begin to build the trust that will lead to recognition. You can then work your way out to the customers and the competitors.

When you are creating a brand, you need to be consistent in everything that you do. Remember, your brand is your image, and inconsistencies will poorly impact the consumers.

The primary question that you should ask yourself is whether or not you deliver everything you promise to your customers. Your answer should always be yes. Delivery on your promises should be consistent at all times.

What is Your Personality?

Your personality has a lot to do with your brand. You should make sure that your personality matches your brand.

It is wise for companies to hire a brand manager so there are not problems with personalities conflicting with a brand. The image of the company needs to be based on what looks good for the company, what is attractive to the customers, and what will sell. Your individual personality should not mix into the brand.

Some people say that you are your brand and your personality should shine through your brand. However, there is a fine line with this theory. A branding manager is a good option because this person can be impartial when he helps you create an image; he will have an unbiased point of view and not allow individual personalities to interfere with the creation of a brand.

Competition

There are many things to consider about your competition when you are designing a branding campaign. Many businesses fail because they do not consider their competition. You need to do proper research on your competitors, learn what makes you different and determine why customers should choose you. Understand that there really is no competition. You never want to look the same as the rest of the companies in your industry. Don't be afraid to step outside of the box and be different. This is how consumers will remember you. If you all look the same, they will think it doesn't matter where they go to make their purchase.

Establishing Brand

Once you have determined your mission and your vision, your audience and your difference from the competitors, you can begin to establish your brand. There are many things that you need to do to establish your brand so people will begin to remember your name. These things include getting inside of the customers' minds, obtaining endorsements, finding hot prospects and using public relations firms to your advantage. These few things will go a long way to establish you in the market.

Establishing a Place Inside of the Customer's Mind

One of your biggest goals in the branding process is establishing a place inside of the customers' minds.

Your goal is to prove to customers that they have a need for your product or for your service. Customers must find a reason why they need you. The branding techniques will tell customers that your product resolves a problem, fulfills a need and makes their life much better. When you get inside the customers' heads, customers will believe they absolutely have to have your product.

Just as you hear many infomercials talk about how someone will become rich if he uses a product or how his health will be better, you need to establish the benefit to the customers so you can make them truly believe that their lives will be much better when they use your product. This also means that you have to build trust and credibility with the customers.

Endorsements

Consumers listen to public figures. When you have the ability to get an endorsement on a product, you need to take advantage of it. However, you cannot wait for an endorsement to come to you.

There are many ways to get endorsements. You may attend events where a public figure is going to be. This includes getting back stage at concerts or shows where you can have access to the person. You also can call celebrities' managers and talk to them about getting an endorsement for your product.

One thing to keep in mind about endorsements is that you need to find someone who matches your audience. If your target audience is teenagers, you want to find an endorsement that the teenagers know and trust.

Find someone who the teenagers think is hip; they will want your product when they learn their idol uses it. The last thing you want to do is get a product endorsement from an older individual, even one who is well known and respected by an older audience, whom the teenage audience has never heard of. This would be a waste of money and time.

Using Public Relations Pro's to Your Advantage

Media attention needs to be used to your advantage. There are many ways to do this. One thing to keep in mind is that your product and your brand do not have to be fully established to gain the attention of the media. You can use the media to help you get established.

Using press releases is one of the best things you can do to get the exposure you are looking for and to help you create a place in the industry. A press release is usually used for announcing grand openings for new businesses, new product launches, big sales and events, or anything else new that is happening within a company.

The elements of a press release should include the event itself; why people will benefit going to it; and the location, date, and time of the event. If you don't tell people where to go, it will do you no good. You should also provide your company contact information in case the media wants to call you to get an interview or to write a story on the company. Customers may have questions. No contact information could cost you a lot of business.

Also, always include your website address in a press release so people can go to your site and learn more about who you are.

Press releases are sent out to as many media outlets as possible to target the audiences you are trying to reach. These media outlets include news stations, newspapers, magazines, radio stations, and more.

When a media outlet receives a press release, they may do a few things. They may immediately respond and use it for the next big story that hits the press. They may put it aside for a while and then use it when they need a story. Alternatively, they may do nothing at all.

Sending out a press release doesn't cost a business anything. It is cheap, and it is always good to send a few out, even if the media is not interested. The point is that you must, at least, try to use public relations to your benefit. It may be only one event or announcement you have about your business that is used by the press. That one small bit of exposure could go a long way for you.

Establishing Company Identity

Establishing your identity is very important when you are fighting for a place in a market or in a certain niche. You may know exactly who you are, but you need to get your name out there for others to be aware of your existence. There are many ways you can establish an identity in a local community or around the world.

Giving Free Information

Many companies upset customers because they want to charge money for everything. This leaves customers walking away with a bad taste in their mouths and only causes the company to look dishonest or greedy. There are things that you can give away for free, especially when it comes to information. You cannot, however, teach a customer everything you know in just a few minutes of talking to them or in a few pages that they can read. Many businesses practice giving free tips and advice through flyers and brochures.

You may want to place a few useful tips on the back of your brochure. This will help build credibility and trust with customers, demonstrating that you are not greedy and are willing to help them achieve certain goals. It will also prove to them that you actually have the knowledge to perform certain tasks within your company. You don't have to reveal secrets of the trade, but you can give out helpful information that is useful.

Giving useful information, for example, may include offering tips and advice when you are out on a service call in a home. If your company offers plumbing services and you are on a call for frozen pipes under a home, you may recommend the customer leave the water dripping overnight. This type of advice is useful to customers and will help them avoid a burst pipe.

You may think it will not benefit you to tell them how to avoid problems because then they won't need you. However, there are plenty of other reasons they can call you. Plus, you will be the person they will turn to any time they need something repaired. In addition, word of mouth goes a long way with customers, and that happy customer may attract you plenty of business.

Adding Value to Your Business

When you are branding, it is important to add value with everything you do. Adding value means making yourself valuable to the customers and the community. This may include giving out free information through tips and tricks, statistics, and other useful bits of information.

You can make the business more valuable by adding a little extra in everything that you do. A voice mail message might include a quick tip on fixing something or a way to prevent a computer virus. The signature on your email should contain more than your name, address and phone number. You might include a useful sentence underneath that is a quick tip or useful bit of information.

Making yourself useful adds value to your business and to the customers' perception of you. The customers must believe that they need you; this is a part of proving to them you are useful and the best person to turn to when they need something.

Media Consideration

The media is extremely important when branding a business. There are many different outlets and each can be used to your advantage, even for damage control. Proper branding means staying connected with the media. Make the media your friend. Some say to keep your friends close and your enemies closer; this is true with the media. They can make you very popular or they can ruin you. There is really no in-between. You need the media on your side at all times.

Local Media

There are many local media outlets you might consider using when you are looking to brand your company or your products. You can use local newspapers to announce sales and events. The television stations are useful when running advertisements or announcing events on the news.

One thing to keep in mind is that public television stations are free; they cannot charge you money to run something on them. If you are a non-profit organization looking to brand your organization, the best way to do it is through public television stations. You can announce events like blood drives and other events on public television. This is great exposure, and it is free.

Other forms of local media may be local websites for town members. Some towns have a site for the community (such as AmericanTowns.com) where people can post things like classified ads and upcoming events. They are free sites and, because of this, are sometimes used more than the newspapers.

Article Writing

Another way you can use the media to your advantage is to write your own articles and distribute them to the press. This is very beneficial. If the press comes across times they need to fill additional space in their paper, they may use them.

Sending articles to the press is free. They will not charge you to use your articles. If you write useful articles to magazines in the industry in which you work, you may even get paid for the articles. Article writing is a very beneficial way to advertise your business, and it helps with the branding process.

Sponsors

Looking for sponsors is very important.

It is very similar to getting an endorsement. You may make a deal with companies to sponsor you; such a deal might include putting up their advertisement at a local event or charity you are holding.

You should always look for local or national sponsors. Sponsors can be used on your website and at your business location. The most common way to obtain sponsors is by offering them advertising for their business.

Sponsors need to see a benefit in it for them, and, if they do, they are usually willing to work with you. Finding local sponsors helps you build credibility with your business.

Written Testimonials

Written testimonials are very important in the branding process because they work in two ways. They help build credibility and trust with the targeted audience. When you sell products or services, it is important to gather as many written testimonials from your customers as you can. A customer can write up the type of product or service he purchased from your company and his experience working with you. The more written testimonials you have, the better.

Written testimonials are beneficial because they create hype. They increase the excitement about your business and make people want to try your product. Testimonials tell the public that you followed through on delivering the promise you made. Importantly, this shows you are reliable and consistent. It shows that you deliver.

Special Offers

Building a brand also requires you to provide offers and special discounts to the customers.

Customers are always looking for a great deal, and when they know they can get it from you, they will shop from you. You might offer discount codes to customers for specific items or even a "buy one get one free" deal. These are excellent ways to promote a business. If you have an online company, you may offer free shipping or other types of discounts during specified periods of time.

Special offers work very well with customers. Free items usually work the best because customers find that very little is ever free. Although it is not cost effective to give away free items, you may include something free with a purchase of a bigger item.

Referrals

Another media consideration when you are building up your brand is that you need to work on obtaining referrals. Referrals work very well in building up your brand. Referrals are the word of mouth endorsements from customers who swear by you. These can be difficult to build, but referrals help in establishing your credibility.

You can help with gaining referrals to your business by offering specials or discounts to customers that refer you to other customers.

This may be a $5 discount on their next purchase or something similar. When customers see there is a benefit in it for them, they will often times refer your company to others to gain the benefit. This helps increase a customer base, revenues and brand awareness.

The Competitive Edge

Creating a competitive edge is another important aspect of branding. Today, the online world has many methods of branding. The most popular method of branding and gaining the competitive edge is through the use of blogs.

Blogs allow a site to increase traffic, to improve rank through search engine results and even to help with building credibility.

About Blogs

Blogs are websites that use the new Web 2.0 technology, which allows visitors to a site to post their own comments, articles and feedback. Giving users access to post comments to your site allows them to feel a sense of ownership in your business. Blogs work in many ways, which may include forums and discussion boards, or they sometimes look like a daily diary. They keep visitors up-to-date on current events and allow for discussion to take place.

Reasons to Use Blogs

There are many reasons to use blogs for a business. A business may want to provide a discussion board that allows other customers to discuss troubleshooting tips and tricks. A company may post useful information about how to get the most longevity out of products, how to repair or fix things, and even how to prevent problems.

Using a Blog to Your Benefit

If you decide to add a blog to your company site, there are many things to consider so you get the most out of it. Some companies allow people to post their own content. The content on your blog should include your important keywords and phrases, links, useful product or service information, and contact information.

The primary purpose of blog writing for branding is to gain more exposure for a business and get the word out to people that the company exists. Blogs are an excellent way to create hype and exposure because the web has millions of businesses and customers.

When using a blog, it is essential to make sure that you use important keywords that are relevant to the products and services offered by your business. These keywords and phrases should be the words that will be typed into the search engines when a user is looking for what you offer. The keywords should be used naturally throughout the content of the blog. They will work by allowing your blog to be pulled up in the search engine results when users type in the specific keywords and phrases you used in the blog.

Adding links to blogs is a very important thing for two reasons. They provide an easy method to get back to your site, and they provide an inbound link. Users always appreciate an easy way to get to your company. Talking in a blog about products and services offered without links to where the customers can find them will not be helpful. Customers will only search for a business for a very short time. You have a better chance of getting new customers when a link is right there in the blog so they can easily click on it and find out more about the company.

URLs are also beneficial for a business because they provide inbound links. One of the ways that search engines work is that they rank a business by popularity. Popularity can be built up by links integrated within blogs.

The more inbound links you provide in a blog, the more popularity a search engine thinks you have. Never forget to place inbound links inside the content you place on your blog.

A blog needs to provide beneficial information for the visitors and readers. When there is something useful to the readers, they will come back for more. Blogs also give you the opportunity to give free advice and useful information that will benefit users and cause you to gain credibility for being knowledgeable about the products and services offered.

Remember, your brand is represented by your ;

Accomplishments

Values

Passions

Vision

Purpose

> *"I am a great believer in luck...*
> *The smarter I work, the more I have."*
> **Mark Zupo – 2001**

More importantly, instead of "Who do **you** think you are?" the question may be better stated as "Who do **they** think you are?" Who you are is reflected in who you are perceived to be. Your presence is fortified by charisma and is a direct reflection of your character. If your **charisma is genuine,** it is always a reflection of your **character.**

Charisma without Character

If you have charisma without character, it's only a matter of time before people find you out. So what is it about a **strong, honest character** that is so important to charisma? Consider the following truths about character:

-Character Lasts

There was a time when people who lacked integrity stood out from the crowd. Now the opposite is true – charisma can make you stand out for a moment as a "flash in the pan" or "flavor of the week," but character will set you apart for a lifetime.

-Character is Trustworthy

Some people are actually suspicious of charisma. Having good character, however, inspires trust. Couple trust with charisma and you become a force that others want to be around.

-Charismatic Behavior Inspires Character

If you lead people, your good character sets a standard for everyone who is following you. People can't emulate your charisma, but they can aspire to your character. If leaders compromise their standards, cheat the company or take shortcuts, so will their followers. And no amount of charisma can make that situation right.

-Character Toughs It Out

During the rough times, which all leaders face; character has the ability to carry you through, which is something that charisma can never do. When you are weary and inclined to quit, **the self-discipline of character** keeps you going.

-Character Is In It for the Long Haul

Charisma, by its nature, doesn't extend very far. It usually produces a quick, blinding light, but then it's gone. Character, on the other hand, is more like a bonfire. Its effects are long-lasting. It produces warmth and light, and as it continues to burn, it gets hotter, providing fuel that burns brighter.

-Character Makes Things Easier

If you're currently leading people, you probably have some measure of both charisma and character. The question is which one are you relying on to lead? The answer can be found in your response to this great question:

"As time goes by, does it get easier or harder to lead?"

Without character, charisma becomes harder to sustain. You constantly have to entertain to get people to notice you. But with character, your influence strengthens, builds, and continues to attract people over time. And best of all, the ones who do come to enjoy your fire stay with you a lot longer than the ones who only want to see a show.

Success Equation:

Charisma + Character = Success

Reputation Management

An individual's reputation is relative. Your reputation is relative to your actions, your visibility, your influence and your intentions. Your brand is your reputation. A person can have great power and control that is achieved by creative deception. A person can deceive the masses with smooth talk and promises that will never be delivered.

One can be powerful and in command of others due to the *perception* that they are in charge. We can be deceived into believing in the promises of those who appear to be genuine. There is a difference, though, between deception and perception.

"Choose your friends wisely; We are most like the five people we are closest to."
Mark Zupo - 2009

- **Deception:** The intention to deceive, a fraud. A trick or an imposter.

  An imposter who presents himself as though he has authority and credibility is often discovered soon after he commands power and takes control. Sometimes it is too late and the result is at the expense of those around him. These imposters' control is never long lasting or of much value.

- **Perception: 1.** The act or faculty of comprehending by means of the senses or of the mind; cognition; understanding. **2.** Immediate or intuitive recognition or appreciation, as of moral, psychological, or aesthetic qualities; insight; intuition; discernment: *an artist of rare perception.* **3.** The result or product of perceiving, as distinguished from the act of perceiving; percept.

"Every drop of water is just as wet as any other drop of water."
Mark Zupo - 2007

When the people around us have a perception of which we are, we must be forthright with our explanation of which we truly are, what we stand for and what it may mean to others. Our explanation must be clear and precise because it will be a valuable instrument in our tool chest, especially when we represent that we have something that is of value to them.

Notice that the definition of perception contains words like quality, insight, intuition, discernment, appreciation and morals. These are the valuable traits that we deliver when we present ourselves to others to gain their trust and confidence. When people hear my name, what do they think of first? What value do I lend to those around me? Do I have a persona?

This is important

The next several chapters detail how you can turn your life into big business. Sit up, pay attention and use what you will learn!

Now we get down to business. Read every detail carefully and take notes.

Here you will find the "blueprint" to take opportunity and turn it into profit!

This is opportunity knocking!

Chapter 5

Building Your Life Product

Turn You into "The Product <u>YOU</u>"
-The Method

The method for turning your life into a product contains a few simple steps that involve a bit of technology and a bit of salesmanship. First you must learn what makes people wealthy and what keeps people wealthy.

- **What can I do to make a living?**

- **What do I know that will make me a living?**

First- ***You Have To <u>Teach People to Give You Money!</u>***

The wealthy people of this world are different. In fact, they are dramatically different from the masses, which is what separates them from you. The one thing they know is that they have to teach people to give them money! Sounds crazy, right? No, not at all.

Wealthy people know the **seven** rules of attaining and retaining wealth:

1. Be decisive.
2. Be prudent.
3. Be responsible.
4. Be receptive to work that drives income.
5. Be generous by helping others attain wealth.
6. Be wary of luck without purpose.
7. Be voluntary. Ask and accept money as your reward.

What the rich learned was never taught in any school. The educational systems in America produce expectations. This is a sort of unconscious dependency on the system to provide for and to care for you instead of allowing you to produce for yourself. That is the exact opposite of entrepreneurship.

School is the first place that teaches you a form of measurement that inhibits your progress and growth as an independent person. The system is designed to let you know how they think you are doing, instead of allowing you to determine how you are doing.

An opposing theory formulates the entrepreneurial mindset, and that is for you to determine what you consider real solutions to real problems.

This fosters imaginative thinking and ingenuity, the skills that are necessary for survival in the real world, as well as for survival in the business world. Being judged for work you don't like causes you to be obsessed with results and grading. It removes the joyful aspect of the process.

7 Money NO's

1. I'm bad with money.
2. Money doesn't grow on trees.
3. Only the rich get richer.
4. Money corrupts people.
5. Rich people are evil.
6. Money is hard to come by.
7. Money is the root of all evil!

- Running the Business of "You"

- **Incorporate You**
- **Monetize You**
- **Create Your Business Plan**
- **Create Your Systems**
- **Name Your Board of Directors**

To begin with, you must have a plan to run the "You" business to achieve the goals you set for yourself.

A goal without a plan is just a wish."
Mark Zupo – 2010

7-LevelSuccess1-2-3™

The First Step in the process is to have a means for people to find you. In this ever-changing world of technology, it is more important for people to find you in the easiest, fastest and most efficient way possible...via the Internet.

You must have a webpage that is the domain of "your name".

Specifically, you need something like mine, http://www.MarkZupo.com. Check out my main website and see what I mean. It is all about me and what I do. You can and should have your own website with your name.

The Second Step in the process is to have a product or products to sell: products that are specifically yours and no one else's, products that define who you are, what you're about or what you represent.

-If You Have a Speech...

"If you have a speech...write it down; you have a book. If you have a book...market it; you have credibility.

If you have credibility...develop it; you have authority. If you have authority...protect it; you have income for life."

Mark Zupo - 2010

If you have ever been to a presentation at a convention center, a hotel meeting room or at a social function, you have heard someone speak about a topic that often seeks to separate you from your money. The topic isn't the important issue here. The presentation is.

When you listened to some person speak, you might have said to yourself, "I could have done that!" The speaker was poor, the speech was poor and the message was worse yet. The presentation skills of the speaker left a lot to be desired and you certainly could have done just as well or even better, right?

The point is, given the same opportunity; you can do the same presentation and, with some guidance and a little professional help, do it even better. The real point is that you can be paid handsomely for it. The only thing separating you from those of authority and credibility is visibility.

Someone who has written a book is automatically perceived to be an authority just because he wrote a book, any book about any topic! The easiest way to write a book is to write on a topic that is dear to you, a passion or something that you know a great deal about.

Presto...you have just become a member of an elite group of authors. You are now recognized as a credible source of information and an authoritative source because...you said so!

When Mohammed Ali was asked, "Why do you think you are the world's greatest boxer?" He replied, "Because...I said so!"

Your first assignment is to write a book. There is a book in everyone. There are huge benefits to writing a book. Just about every famous person you have ever heard of either became famous because he wrote a book or became more famous because he wrote a book. Just pick a name of someone you know that is famous and see what the title of his book is. I am sure he has one.

It doesn't matter what industry, what walk of life or what subject, be it political, religious, social or business; a book has been written by someone who has made money on it.

A book makes you an expert. It makes you an authority. A book establishes you as a credible source. There is no other medium that can deliver the results a book can. Your book makes you stand out in a world of experts because you are an authority in your industry or in your area of expertise.

Some examples are

- Robert Kiyosaki wrote *Rich Dad Poor Dad* and was virtually unknown until he wrote a book.
- Brendon Burchard wrote *Life's Golden Ticket* and was virtually unknown until he wrote a book.
- Tom Clancy wrote *The Hunt for Red October* and was virtually unknown until he wrote a book.
- Timothy Ferriss wrote *The Four Hour Work Week* and was virtually unknown until he wrote a book.

A book, with a mere mention of it on the right media platform such as CNN, Oprah and the like, can propel you to national recognition. Once you get noticed, your name and business will take on a life of its own.

Your book is used as ---

- ✓ **A Tool be recognized**
- ✓ **A Door Opener**
- ✓ **A Business Card**
- ✓ **A Method to Charge More Based on Perception**
- ✓ **A Device to Generate Revenue**
- ✓ **A Means to Develop Multiple Streams of Income**

Here is an example of how I help other people write their books *FAST!* This is an advertisement for my program that helps you develop a book. Check out my program to help you write your book with lightning speed. It is called:

YourFastBook. In the "YourFastBook™" workshop, you'll learn:

- How to write your book without ever putting pen to paper!

- How to market your book without ever paying a publisher!

- How to make your book available to millions with a click of a button!

- How to avoid the 10 most common mistakes authors make!

- How to protect yourself with this simple free technique!

- How never to pay a royalty and keep all the profit for yourself!

Don't Spend Years Trying to Write Your Book!

There is a Fast and Painless Way to Write a Book without having to actually write it Word for Word!

The Secrets to Writing & Selling Your First Book Fast!

The Original How to "Write and Sell Your First Book" Workshop

Saturdays, 11-5

Have you ever thought of writing a book, but you just can't find the time? Now you can...because I will show you how to do it faster than you ever thought possible!

The **"YourFastBook™"** Workshop will give you all the tools you'll ever need to "blast" out a book in no time flat!

Still Not Convinced?

I am the author or co-author of more than 23 books to date.
I am a "top-selling" author and credible authority on the self-publishing secrets that conventional industry publishers don't want you to know.

Check this out! When you enroll in my award-winning workshop you'll get all this and more:

- How to write your book in one day!
- How to give your book an award-winning title!
- The three secrets to every author's success with future orders!
- How to turn your book into a "Money-Machine"
- How to make people pay five times what you paid for printing!
- Why the best books never get published and are lost forever!
- How to develop multiple streams of income from your book.

The Third Step in the process is to develop your database, which is a list of people that follow you on social media websites like Twitter, Facebook, LinkedIn, and YouTube.com™ and so on. You can develop a database by offering a free informational product in exchange for an email address.

This may be the most important step in the process of selling you as a product. This strategy works very well and great attention should be paid to these steps to get the maximum outcome from it. Why will this work so well for you? Aligning yourself with an already respected marketer or easily recognized authority gives the impression of credibility based upon that association.

These authorities and celebrities in the business world may also have established lists of their own that can be "rented" to you in exchange for some consideration. You can see evidence of this with Taco Bell and Kentucky Fried Chicken restaurants in the same building.

There can be a shared promotional opportunity between you and another recognized person or company. The association gives an implied endorsement of you and your products.

Once you have focused on a market to direct your campaign and you have developed a product to sell, you then begin to collect partners who are willing to promote you and your products.

Then you establish a list of their clients to market to for shared exposure or profit. When you enlist new partners to help drive traffic to you, you establish and maintain the new list of patrons from that point on.

Any new interested opt-ins, those who opt to receive information about you and your products, are seeking to satisfy their own curiosity. Some will stay and some will go. If you deliver great content, products or services, you will get great things in return.

Here are seven simple steps to successfully building and monetizing a list:

1. Specifically define your target market.

Define, with precision and specificity, who you are selling to.

2. Create an irresistible lead-generating magnet.

Get their attention and deliver unbelievable value.

3. Create an email marketing campaign.

Capture and store permission-based opt-ins.

4. Convert your new leads from an opt-in squeeze page.

Publish a squeeze page that hits hard and demands action.

5. Drive traffic to your opt-in page with social media.

Use social media in every form to direct attention to your site.

6. Instill sincerity and trust in your new list of interested opt-ins.

Build trust, establish credibility and maintain authority and respect.

7. Monetize your list with front and back-end sales.

Solve their problems. Create, promote and sell what they want. Offer more; offer it again.

The point of establishing your own list is to market to those on it forever. Let's do some simple math to establish just how important everyone is to you. Every subscriber you have collected who pays you $10 dollars will add up to a thousand dollars very quickly.

For example:

1- A subscriber pays you **$29 dollars** a month.

2- More subscribers pay you **$29 dollars** and do so for month after month.

3- New subscribers pay you **$29 dollars** and add to your database of people who will buy more from you down the road.

Let's look at this example:

Add this up: You get 50 subscribers to your newsletter or program. Once you have 50 subscribers, multiply each of them by $29. That equals **$1,450 dollars**...a <u>month!</u> When you have 50 customers who have bought from you once, you can market other products to them over and over again.

A second example: You already have $1,450 dollars a month from them. Now, sell one or more products to them as well. Let's say you sell three additional products at $24 each.

3 additional products - 25 X $24 dollars = **$600 dollars**...a month!

Now you have a possible additional **$600 a month**.

Consider this: $600 dollars plus $1,450 dollars = **$2,250 dollars**...a month! All this comes from selling to people once. This can be repeated many times over.

One key strategy they use is to up-sell you, to suggest upgrades and more expensive products, almost immediately after you have made a purchase.

As you can see, the earnings will add up very fast to a point when you couldn't stop it if you tried. Imagine if your first product was priced at $39 dollars or $47 dollars instead of $24?

These are people you may never meet individually and pay you a small amount but collectively they pay you a great deal of money.

Do The Math!

Chapter 6

Marketing Yourself

**Spread the word about you with
The Four Step Process to Selling You:**

1. Positioning

Positioning is the requirement that you establish yourself as an authority or an expert. What is the process for that? You establish your authority or expertise based upon your experience and education in an area in which other people aren't as skilled. You can read as few as twenty books on any subject. You can say confidently that you know more about that subject than most of the people in the country. Once you're established in a field, if it is in print, it is generally believed simply because it is in print. This is how you establish your authority.

2. Packaging

Packaging yourself is a simple matter of recording your presentations in one form or another and placing them on digital formats, book text formats and audio formats, such as a CD, a DVD, a book or an Mp3 recording.

3. Promoting

Promoting yourself can be a challenge; however, it has and can be done effectively. There are many means, through radio advertising and radio interviews, television interviews and print mentions. There are my favorites as well, such as webinars, Tele-seminars, word of mouth and more.

4. Partnering

Partnering is simply a joint venture between you and another like-minded person or company. You could choose to "piggyback" your advertising or information to be promoted on another person's list. This is a very effective method for someone without a starting list of his own.

5. Authoring

The next step is to write a book. Writing a book gives you an unbelievable amount of credibility simply because of what most people see as the complexity of writing a book. That, in itself, is a huge accomplishment for most people. Soon, you'll learn that it is an easy process you can accomplish in a short amount of time. You'll also see that it is probably the one single thing that you can do to enhance your credibility, authority and recognition. Once you have committed to writing a book, your focus is to market it. Marketing is the absolute key to your success as an author. Just ask any publisher what the biggest costs are associated with your book and he will tell you marketing. It costs pennies to actually print your book and thousands to market it.

If the traditional publisher doesn't think your book will generate a substantial income, you will never get published! I am sure you have heard the nightmare tales of an author submitting hundreds of manuscripts in hopes of being published, only to be turned down as many times!

Today, through technology and automation, the game has changed. It is now possible to draft, write, transcribe, print and sell a book in less-than 30 days!

-Social Networking the Globe

3-V's of Communication

1. Verbal   7%

2. Vocal   38%

3. Visual   55%

"Early to bed and early to rise...
work like hell and advertise!"
- Ted Turner

Think Marketing, Marketing, Marketing......

There are only <u>three</u> ways of building wealth today:

- You can either take a one-time job and **get paid once a week for every week you work** (after you work).
- You can work-for-hire (contract), which is usually limited to a one-time deal.
- You can build your own business and earn **residual income**...virtually forever!

The last method is obviously the most desired method of building wealth, earning residual income whereby you can earn <u>over and over</u>, even though you only put in the effort once!   Let me repeat that...***ONCE!***

Actors, writers, musicians, singers and inventors are marketers who earn residual income from their past accomplishments. Those accomplishments pay them virtually forever, and yours should too!

There are a few recurring income secrets you can learn that, as soon as you put them into practice, will change your life forever. The great thing about them is that they are much easier than what you are doing now.

The secret I will reveal to you is…<u>it is no secret</u>. That's right. It is a simple process of marketing that the rich study and that the wealthy have put into practice. This is the same method that you can use too.

It starts with

- ✓ **Duplicating Yourself**
- ✓ **Marketing yourself**
- ✓ **Marketing What You Know**

Duplicating Yourself

7-Secrets to Profit from Your Executive Life Experience!

System-ate. Automate, Delegate, Replicate

1. Do you have a Message?

Everyone has a story to tell and some have a few more than that. If you can put your message into an outline format and present it to more than one person, you have a speech!

2. Who are you?

Are you a person others look up to? Are you a person who leads other people? If you are, you have the ability to teach others and delegate tasks that help spread the word about your message.

3. What are you?

Are you a person with the ability to speak, to present, to organize thoughts and processes? If so, you can take your knowledge and experience and put it into an automatic system to help other people...for a price.

4. What is your purpose?

Are you driven to deliver your message because it makes you feel better and it helps other people? Are you motivated by fame or success or by the confidence that you will make a difference? If so, coaching others is absolutely for you.

5. What are your passions?

Is there something that you have always been passionate about? Is it something that drives you, the very thing that you live for? If so, you have knowledge and experience that someone else with the same passions may lack in their endeavors.

6. What can you do for others?

What is the one thing that you know that you can share with others that would improve their lives? What is it you have discovered that has been withheld from people, the information that would make a difference in their lives if they just had the knowledge?

Knowing that your simple offer of information has the power to change a life will reward you with confidence in yourself. That reward, however, is small compared to the reward of satisfaction you'll receive knowing you've made a significant impact on someone else's life. "Can you help me? Can you help me help myself?" If so, coaching is for you.

7. What do you have to offer that is of value?

Is it possible that you know something that would be of great value to someone else - even if you think it is so simple that you never give it a second thought?

The concept of value is in how useful the information is that you give. How the value of that information is credited in another person's mind is based on what it does for him.

The information that contains the highest

value is determined by the person who gets it, not the person that gives it. That said; never underestimate the value of your knowledge or experience, no matter how small it seems to you.

Social Media: **What is my "Web-inality?" Do I have a social image?**

You can make money helping other people!

- Can you package your message?
- Can you change someone's life?
- Can you inspire someone's life?
- Can you motivate someone else to greatness?

Chapter 7

Building a Membership / Mentoring what You Know

-Coaching [This one is HOT]

Lead, Follow or Get Out of the Way!

Deliver impactful information from your life's experience.

Question? Can your education or experience in a specific area or industry be used to help other people solve their problems?

Question? Will your helping people to solve their problems bring you some satisfaction or reward?

Question? Does a market who is willing to pay for what you know exist?

Question? Can you feel satisfied taking money from people by selling what seems, to you, to be simple information? Consider that you could generate a few hundred, to many thousands, of dollars a month.

If this is something that you can conceive doing, then you have just made an important step in turning what you know into a business!

There are six basic steps to the process. Let's get started.

-The "How To" to it.

Step 1. Create an Outline

List what you know, your expertise or your passion in an outline that you could teach to clients. If your education or experience is in fundraising, list the forms of fundraising. List the timeline the coaching will require. Then list the responsibilities. Next, list the methods and pricing. You get the idea.

Step 2. Structure Your Program

Coaching is a methodical process and can be time consuming. It is very important that you form a schedule which details your availability and the length of lessons, etc. Make your schedule fit your own timeline and work with clients to adjust a cooperative meeting schedule.

   a. How long will your program last?

   b. What days / time will you meet?

   c. Determine if you will meet one-on-one?

d. Determine if meetings will be in group settings?

e. Determine if your program will be delivered digitally or in person?

Step 3. Set the Price of Your Program

Structure your coaching program pricing to match your expertise and demand. Look around to other coaching programs and coaches to see what market rates are. We'll discuss some examples later.

Most personal authoritative coaches charge between $500 to $1,200 per hour. Experienced coaches may charge by the person or session at $2,500   up to $25,000. Note* Some of the highest priced jewelry is almost the same as lesser priced jewelry except that it comes from a "high-priced" business with an iconic name.

You could buy two identical rings, one from Walmart and one from Tiffany's. My guess is that the one from Tiffany's will cost several thousand more dollars...because it came from Tiffany's.

Step 4. Market your Program

Market your coaching program to a select

audience of like-minded people. They will be easy to find once you have established yourself as a credible resource.

   a. Look for problems that need solving.

   b. Use what you know to help others.

   c. Deliver great information and content if you expect to demand high prices.

   d. Be professional and give freely. Abundance and quality are the keys here.

   e. Use email and electronic delivery methods to distribute your sales material.

   f. Always mention your products and services when you speak to others.

   g. Use free webinars and Tele-seminars at every opportunity to pitch your products and services.

   h. Write articles and make comments on other people's blogs and Twitter when applicable.

   i. Distribute FREE reports and eBooks to anyone at every opportunity.

   j. Contribute to forums when you can.

Step 5. Set the Delivery

Set the delivery of your coaching program in any form that works best for you. It can be in a digital webinar, in a Tele-seminar or in person at a local hotel. It can be an audio program or a video program. You can make all of these products from a single source and repurpose each for optimum delivery. We will discuss these options in more detail later on.

    a. Be a teacher, coach and mentor.

    b. Deliver what you know.

Step 6. Continue to Develop

As you present your program, reevaluate it to improve it, update it and advance it for precise timing and your best possible performance. You can lead people to success with your life's authority and experience.

Survey your clients and ask what they want. Ask what they need and what they are looking for in terms of more value and worth.

    Follow those before you who are a success. The most successful businesses in the world that experience the fewest failures are those that are franchised, like McDonald's and Starbucks. Why? Because millions of dollars have been spent to work out the kinks, fix the bugs and correct the mistakes that years of business history have uncovered.

That said, it isn't necessary to buy into a franchise to be a success, but if you watch them and study their tactics and procedures, it is possible to mimic their success.

To the point...there are a lot of people who have said, "If I had only known then what I know now." So now that you know what you always needed to know...why not share it for a profit?

Your Personal "ATM" Coaching Program

This is your plan for authoritative and trusted status as a coach and mentor:

1. Create a quantifiable plan for success.

    a. Set a dollar amount to achieve through your coaching sales.

    b. Set a price such as $197 a month for your book, audio, webinar, Tele-seminar, CD training program or DVD training program. $200 x 12 months

= $2,400 x 100 people = $240,000!!!!!

2. **Build a subscription program for training or coaching.**

   a. 100 people x $97 = $9,700 / month! = $116,400/ year! And…you only have to have one month's content to start! I can show you how to start with only one month's content and then build contents for the following months during the second month!

3. **Develop your product as a premium product limited to select members of an exclusive membership.**

   a. Digitally record a live training session, extract audio from video, etc. Sell the audio and the entire training DVD as a product. Use the audio as a free download to sell the entire package.

b. Turn your presentation into an audio / DVD/, transcription, workbook or slide presentation. Use them to teach others, or allow your mentees access to teach others.

This is also a great source for an affiliate program.

    c. Imagine that you sell (via affiliates) 50 / month @ $497 = $24,850 /month x 12 = $298,200 / year. AND YOU DID NOTHING!

4. **Produce a "big-ticket" COACHING seminar series for selected students (or anyone else for that matter).**
   a. Imagine coaching on a cruise ship! Imagine coaching at a luxury hotel in Las Vegas! 50 tickets at $1,997 seminar = $99,850 / year. This is a one-time event! One night or one two-day weekend! What else can I say?

5. **Create a Coaching Program with a high-value "Executive," "Gold," "Diamond," or "Platinum" group participation.**
       a. 15 people at $2,000 / month = $30,000 / month x 12 = $360,000 / year.

As you can see, the options are endless. The rewards will come to those that have the guts to take the first step! Just imagine...even if you earned a portion of this? Even if you weren't that good? Even if you make mistakes, you will still make more money than you ever have made working for a living, and you'll have a lot more fun in the process.

-How Do I Start?

1. Offer a FREE seminar as close to home as possible so you'll have no travel and no excess fees or expenses.

2. Find a venue, a place you can have it, where you can gather at least 25 to 50 people.

3. Deliver your speech, seminar, information or resources for no less than 60 minutes.

4. Record it to audio.

5. Digitally record it on video, every part of it from the beginning to the end. Get plenty of audience interaction and reaction.

6. Be sure and make a gentle call to action throughout the presentation and at the end. It should be for a personal coaching program, either a one-on-one, group or digital offering.

You're Presentation Agenda

1. Develop you pricing first.
2. Develop your length and process.
3. Get a meeting room or auditorium.
4. Produce your marketing piece, flyer, billboard, poster, etc.

5. Get a sponsor to help with expenses for a return on his help.

6. Get the sponsor to help in distribution of your marketing materials.

7. Offer a FREE strategy session for members and attendees.

8. Use the questionnaire and poll method to close your coaching program and sell even more.

9. Turn your recorded program into a keynote speech, book and info product.

10. Repurpose everything you have into digital form.

The Possibilities

Let's talk about the possibilities of what might be generated from ONE Tele-seminar.

- Deliver a one hour / 60-minute Tele-seminar or webinar.

- Deliver a one hour / 60-minute Tele-seminar or webinar per week.

- Close only TWO sales from ONE Tele-seminar.

Do this on a part-time basis.

One sale @ $497 X 2 = $994 PER WEEK!

That's $3,976 per month!

That's $47,712 PER YEAR>>>>>

PART TIME!

"Rocks need polishing to become gems. Gems need polishing regularly to remain brilliant."

Mark Zupo - 2009

Chapter 8

Leaving a Legacy

How to Re-Package your Life Experience and <u>Sell It For a Profit!</u>

> *"Just because you are sharing an experience with someone else doesn't mean that you are having the same experience."*
> - Mark Zupo – 2010

Your Uniqueness is Your Product!

Here are 15 ways to sell what you know packaged as a product:

1. Books
2. Video Course / Program on DVD
3. Audio Course / Program on CD
4. Digital eBooks
5. Tele-Seminars
6. Webinars
7. Live Seminars
8. Recorded Webinars
9. Affiliate Programs
10. Joint Ventures
11. Fundraisers

12. Corporate Sponsorship
13. Coaching Programs
14. Mentorship Programs
15. Public Speaking

Video

Remember the 3-V's of Communication?

The 3-V's of communication demonstrate that the most important aspect of communication mediums is the visual. At 55%, visual communication is the most successful method to present to prospective buyers.

1. Verbal   7%

2. Vocal   38%

3. Visual   55%

-Introduction to Video Marketing

There is no better way to penetrate your market and get people excited about your offer than with video marketing campaigns. Not only can you exploit the power of video marketing to propel your viewers into taking action, but you can quickly establish a defined brand of your own.

Videos add life to our marketing campaigns. They transform static, traditional campaigns into action-driven presentations that unleash our message in a powerful, dramatic way. Videos also give you the unique opportunity to communicate with your target audience in a way that puts you in touch with what is truly important to them, what motivates them and what will leave an everlasting impression.

However, videos have more value than just providing you with an interactive vehicle for your marketing message. Videos also help to increase the value of your products and of your brand. If you are involved in information marketing, you can instantly ramp up the perceived value of your products by adding in video-based components.

People often learn better when they are given a visual of both their tasks and examples of the end result. Creating dynamic video lessons or tutorials will instantly increase conversion rates and skyrocket your income.

So, now that you understand just how important high quality video presentations are to your marketing message, let's take a closer look at how you can develop laser-targeted video campaigns that speak your customer's language. After all, not all videos are created equally.

-Creating High Quality Videos

Imagine if you were able to personally welcome people to your website, to guide them through your information and to direct them to your order button. Imagine what that would do for your conversion rates! **Well, with videos - that's exactly what you can do.** Who am I? What do I contribute? Why do you need me? Videos can give you a call to action.

You can use videos in a number of different ways, including in sales pitches and tutorials, within your launch sequence to warm up customers and in the development of brand awareness. The more often people see you or hear you, the faster they'll recognize your brand.

The trouble is that many new entrepreneurs struggle with the technical aspects of creating high quality videos. They aren't sure what programs to use, how to edit videos, how to enhance the quality, or even how to create scripts or motions that guide viewers from one frame to another, retaining their attention every step of the way.

The great news is that even if you have absolutely no experience creating videos, there are tools and resources you can use to develop high quality, interactive videos in a matter of a few short hours. For starters, the majority of new computers come bundled with video production software already. However, if you really want to ramp up the quality of your videos, you'll want to consider purchasing an industry grade program, such as Camtasia™ or CamStudio™. These programs will help to add functionality to your videos, while making it easy for you to integrate sound (audio narratives, music, etc.), as well as to highlight important notes and to provide you with added flexibility in editing video content.

"Passion is the key...sharing is the path."

Mark Zupo - 2010

Own it...Live it...Believe it...Teach it

Characteristics of High Achievers:

- Have specific and measurable goals
- Take responsibility for their actions
- Want feedback to make improvements
- Share goals with those who can help them achieve
- Concentrate on high-payoff activities
- Prospect new markets and opportunities
- Set activities on a daily calendar
- Follow up on tasks, assignments and mission
- Review goals frequently to remain focused
- Emulate success in every detail

Chapter 9

Write, Publish and Sell Your Life Story

Turning Your Lifelong Experience into Lifelong Income

What does each of the following categories have in common?

(Expert, Authority, Servant-Leader, Author, Speaker, Coach, Seminar Leader, Online Marketer)

Each is a vehicle for you to capitalize on your experience and knowledge. Each is best expressed in a manner that most everyone can understand…**in writing**. The most effective vehicle for delivering your experience and knowledge is a book. A book is a tried and true, trusted vehicle that is accepted by everyone.

Being a published author serves to spread the word about you and your gifts. It adds instant credibility and trust. There has never been a better business card than a book written by you. There is nothing that establishes authority like authorship and nothing that establishes credibility like a speaker. The more interesting consideration is you can also capture the recognition and advantages that come from speaking when you extend the reach of your message through writing. A book will help establish you as a recognized expert in your field.

The foundation for your recognition and success is in a book and a speech. It comes from an honest account of your life experiences, education and knowledge. **You have experiences and knowledge worth a fortune!**

There isn't anyone who doesn't have a story worth telling. Will you deliver a message that will improve people's lives, change their lives and empower them to action?

Questions to ask yourself:

Do you have a passion that you can share?

1. What excites you?
2. What would other people like to know about you?
3. How would someone's life be changed by your message?

4. Can you accept earning a good living sharing your message?

Would you like to write a book?

1. Is there a book waiting to pour out of you?
2. Have you ever tried to write your thoughts down?
3. Have you ever studied how to write a book?
4. Do you know how a book can help you?

Would you like to be a speaker?

1. Have you ever made a presentation to a group?
2. Could you present to people in your industry?
3. Are there people anxious to know how you can help them?
4. Has anyone asked to hear your story?

The one thing I learned long ago is that to be as good as the experts is to learn directly from the people who have done what I want to do. There is no need to reinvent the wheel. That's why I started **The Mind Your Business™ Seminars to help others find their**

expertise and develop their own successes.

The Mind Your Business™ Seminars will teach you how to present your message and find the right path for reaching your audience. You will have the tools you need to establish a personal message brand and to generate income from your message.

Starting with how to distinguish yourself in the marketplace, you'll learn how to demonstrate your uniqueness, how to create additional income by learning how to write your own book and how to deliver highly effective presentations of your message.

Our expert workshop is designed to help you:

- Become a speaker to promote yourself, your products and your services.
- Build a loyal database of ideal clients and followers.
- Become an author and an authority in your industry or niche.
- Perfect the process to turn your passion into profits.
- Build an online presence and develop the "Product You."

- Build immediate income to fund your projects and lifestyle.

I've had the privilege of helping many people just like you to cash in on their message and to establish their expert status as a sought-after authority.

This is the best and most exciting time in the history of the economic world. A new breed of information-entrepreneurs is using the vehicles of social networking, audio and video technologies, print media and other offline methods to build massive productions for their life's purpose and passion.

Mind Your Business Seminars™ gives you field-tested techniques for establishing yourself as an expert using your book idea and speaking abilities to open up opportunities to share your message.

Here's what you will learn about your book:

- How to find a title, subject and niche for your book
- Secret methods for creating a book in a few short days

- Self-Publishing tips to ensure maximum control and distribution of your book to information-hungry buyers
- Techniques for getting your book in front of the right people at the right time for the right price
- Methods for repurposing your book and expanding your brand
- Promotion techniques to leverage your maximum return

Here is what you'll learn about speaking:
- How to create the Seminar Checklist that ensures your success
- The greatest topic and title that drives in readers and followers
- The best days and times to book a speaking gig or seminar
- How to deliver a totally awesome presentation that kicks BUTT
- What visual methods and presentation aids work
- How to instantly create product from your live presentations

    The **Mind Your Business™** live event is a Super Weekend Workshop jammed with the information necessary to catapult your speaking and writing career into orbit.

    The **Mind Your Business™** training resources are available so that after attending a live event, you can continue to learn in the comfort of your home or office. Everyone has an individual learning style that fits. We appreciate your preferred learning style and the time you can commit, so we have the content and experts to help you through our **7-Level Success Mentorship Program**™ to help you become the in-demand expert in your niche.

The **7-Level Success Mentorship Program**™ is delivered as a monthly webinar, seminar, Tele-seminar or audio program that delivers all the necessary information you will need as you need it. It is a step-by-step process to ensure that you master each step to make the next step a success.

You owe it to yourself to have every chance to make your success happen. Great **opportunities** for entrepreneurs exist right now and have never been better. There is no excuse not to take advantage of the opportunities that lie ahead of you to achieve the success you've been dreaming about.

Here are some tips to get you started on your self-published book:

"Make Your Business Your Life and Make Your Life Your Business!"
- Mark Zupo 2010

7-Level Success Mentorship Program™
Seminars

Chapter 10

Your computer – Your personal "ATM"

Self-Publishing your book

-Idea Producer One: What you're good at.

Make a list of 20 things you're good at. Don't think too hard about this. Maybe you're good at buying presents for people—you've got a knack for choosing just the right gift. Maybe you're a good cook or a good parent or a good swimmer or a good tennis player. Or maybe you used to be good at one or more of these things. For example: I grew up with horses and owned horses for many years. I'm good with horses, and I'm a good rider. If I saw a gap in the market for a horse book, I'd feel comfortable writing the book.

You get the idea. List at least 20 things that you're good at or have been good at in the past. For example, if you know you're an excellent gardener, even though you now live an apartment, list "gardening."

-Idea Producer Two: Your past experiences.

Experiences sell. If you've been abducted by little green men from Mars, it's a book. If you're a bigamist, it's a book. People have written books about their illnesses (see from challenge to opportunity below), their addictions and their pets. Browse through the bestseller lists to see what personal experiences people are writing about.

Don't get bogged down with this; list 20 experiences you've had that spring to mind. The easiest way to come up with experiences is to work backwards through the stages of your life or through decades. Again, don't take a long time over this. Set a time limit --- ten minutes is enough.

-Idea Producer Three: Your knowledge.

What do you know? Start by making a list of all the subjects you were good at in school. Then list all the jobs you've had – yes, part time work counts.

Also list:

- **Your hobbies.** Are you a keen Chihuahua breeder? Do you quilt? Take photographs?

- **Your current job.** What are you learning in your job that other people would pay to learn?
- **The places you've lived.** Your hometown may be boring to you, but guide books sell well.
- **Your family tree.** What special knowledge do your nearest and dearest have that you could write about?

Spend around ten minutes writing down as many subjects as you can that you have knowledge about.

-Idea Producer Four: What you enjoy most.

What do you love? People have written about garage sales, cosmetics, cars and vacations. If you love something, chances are that thousands, or maybe millions, of others will love it too.

Watch the newspapers and take note of current trends. Or better yet, listen to what your children are talking about or asking you to buy for them. Children tend to be up on what's happening.

With some education and assistance, you can publish a book in just a few days! With the advent of on-demand printing, you can go from concept to book-in-hand in about one week!

This doesn't mean, of course, that you can't write on perennial favorites like money, sex and exercise. These topics never go out of popularity, and a new twist on one of these is always a sure bet. The idea of writing about what you enjoy is that you will be bringing passion and enthusiasm to your topic. Enthusiasm is a must.

-Idea Producer Five: From challenge to opportunity.

You face challenges every day. Most are minor; some are major. If you've ever faced a large challenge, or if you're facing one right now, then consider that the things you learn could help other people. Whatever your challenge is, whether it's moving to a new house or confronting a life-threatening illness, other people face the same challenges, and in those challenges are the seeds of books.

Make a list of 20 challenges you've faced in your life. Anything catastrophic qualifies: the loss of your job, the threat of bankruptcy, the betrayal of a spouse. If you've had a quiet life, then make a list of challenges that the people you know have faced. Additional challenges you can consider include any habit you've broken, from congenital lateness to overeating. When you've finished brainstorming, you'll have dozens of book ideas. Winnow out the non-starters. Don't delete them; move them to another computer file. Call it "odds and ends" or "snippets."

"Every challenge delivers opportunity. The bigger the challenge...the bigger the opportunity."

\- **Mark Zupo**

Checklist: Is this the right idea for you TODAY?

You've worked through the idea generators, and you have one or more ideas which you feel would work as a book. The next step is to scrutinize your primary idea carefully.

Consider your idea and look at this list of questions. See if you can answer "Yes" to all of them:

- ☑ Am I enthusiastic enough about this subject and my ideas about it to sell this proposal to an agent and an editor – and to readers?

- ☑ Will I retain my enthusiasm in the time it will take me to complete the book?

- ☑ Is there a market for my book? (I've checked Amazon.com and bookshops for competing titles. I'm convinced there is a market for my book.)

- ☑ I can find people with expert knowledge to interview as I write my book.

- ☑ Does my book provide solutions to problems?

If you can answer YES to most of these questions, you're set.

Chapter 11

Your Call to Action

Ignorance on Fire Beats Knowledge on Ice!

There are two important differences between motivation and inspiration. It will become important to learn what they are to lead you to success. I will teach you to understand why:

- You are the Master of Your Success.
- You are the Master of Your Achievements.
- You are the Master of Wealth, Freedom and Happiness.

I believe that there are only three types of people:

1. The type of person that watches things happen.//
2. The type of person that makes things happen.
3. The type of person that asks, "What happened?"

Which are you?

I teach you how to dispel the myths of failure, lack of control, and negative influences of other people. I will teach you how to find your "Real Dream System" to empower you with the strength and desire to "Be All You Can Be" and "All You Want To Be!" If it's been done before, then You can do it too! Be The First To Imagine It, And then...Achieve What You Can Believe!

Here, you will learn three simple goal-setting methods that you can do before you are done brushing your teeth in the morning. You will learn how you can visualize your dreams and make them a reality. You will learn how you can do anything, be anything and achieve anything that anyone else can do, be and achieve.

"Oh, really?" you say. Yes really! If it has been done before, someone just like you did it. So what makes you think that you can't do it? They had money, they had time, they had help, they had....who cares what they had? You have the same resources within your reach and...all you have to do is ask.

When it comes to life and business, it is no coincidence that some people always seem to fail while others always seem to flourish. For sure, chance plays a role in everything. But as individuals, as business-owners, as thinkers and as parents, we have a significant degree of control over our lives.

Now, we can use the control that we have to influence outcomes negatively. Or we can use it to influence outcomes in our favor and in the favor of those we care about most. When we use our control poorly or when we don't use it at all, it should come as no surprise that our outcomes are bad. And when we use our control thoughtfully and carefully, it should be less surprising when we succeed.

Let me give you an example. At work, your employer considers you for a promotion; however, at the same time, she considers several of your co-workers for the same promotion. Now, as many do, you might immediately say, "There's nothing I can do to influence my boss in my favor. Instead, this decision will be determined by things that are out of my control." And, of course, when the day comes, you will not get that promotion. Instead, someone who pushed hard to demonstrate his worthiness for the position will get the job. You will be left wondering why that person is always successful and always gets promotions, raises, and the adoration of management.

You might even feel resentment toward that person, even though you consider him a friend. When it comes down to it, though, it wasn't your friend who caused you to miss the promotion (or at least not to give yourself the best shot at getting it). Rather, it was your own behavior that prevented your boss from seriously considering you as a candidate.

Fortunately for you, this book is all about situations just like the one we described above. It's about feeling powerless when you're not, experiencing bad outcomes when there's no reason to and, finally, about making sure this problem stops.

> ***"A diamond in an ugly setting...***
> ***is still a diamond."***
>
> **Mark Zupo - 2008**

Most importantly, this book is about success. It is about extracting the characteristics of others that make them successful at work, in parenthood or in the workplace, and then adopting those characteristics for your own use.

So, without further ado, let's take the plunge. Today, you will stop telling yourself that you have no control over your life; and today, you will learn exactly what it means to take that control, grasp it firmly and use it to achieve success in all areas of your life. Set a goal, make a plan and DO IT!

"The greatest manifestation of productive effort is celebrated...at the Bank!"

- **Unknown**

Mentorship Programs: Follow the Leader

Learn from a model of success

You need to mentor others to change, create, empower, lead, build, enable, direct and guide others' lives to their specific independence and triumphs.

Mentoring versus Coaching

Definition: Mentor – *noun*

1. A wise and trusted counselor or teacher.

    An influential senior sponsor or supporter.

2. Definition: Coach – *verb/noun*

    To give instruction or advice in the capacity of a coach. A person who gives instruction.

What is a Mentor?

When we think of other people who helped us in our lives because of their experience and expertise or because of their interest or consideration towards us, we think of them as nice people who gave of themselves. We think of them as being kind to us or as helping us reach our goals or expectations. Whenever we were faced with a challenge or problem that seemed too hard for us to fix, those people used their life experiences as guidance to help us. This could have been as a child, in school, at home or even at work. Usually they were keen to point out talents that we didn't know we had or that we had not yet used.

Mentors come in many forms. They are teachers, parents, coworkers, bosses, other students, friends and relatives. In the past, people were mentored personally and in someone else's presence; but today's technology allows for mentoring to take place via many electronic means, and it eliminates the challenges presented by time and distance. The ability to mentor many people at one time via an electronic method is an invaluable tool and actually provides for many more opportunities for the participants. It helps to bring together people from many walks of life and cultural backgrounds.

As a mentor you will deliver the following:

- **Information**

  ✓ A Mentor will share his life and business experience and knowledge.

- **Methodology**

  ✓ A Mentor will deliver a precise and formatted methodology as a template for success.

- **Instruction**

  ✓ A Mentor will direct the mentees with pre-programmed direction and focus.

- **Opportunity**

  ✓ A Mentor will guide the mentee in various forms of opportunity with industry knowledge and experience.

- **Challenges**

  ✓ A Mentor will challenge and stimulate curiosity while building confidence and trust.

- **Support**

✓ A Mentor will build trust and achievement through his support.

- **Guidance**

✓ A Mentor will use his or her experience to guide the mentee in a focused and direct course to achieve the best outcome.

- **Goals and Expectations**

✓ A Mentor will give guidance and help to open lines of communication while defining a mentee's goals and objectives.

- **Advice**

✓ A Mentor will guide and help a mentee in reaching goals.

- **Models of Success**

✓ A Mentor will change, create, share, empower, lead, build, enable, direct and guide the lives of his mentees to their specific independence and triumphs.

Mentor Program Guidelines

A mentorship program offers a mentee the unique opportunity to develop a relationship with a mentor who is more experienced and skilled in the area that he wants to learn about. A mentor's experiences, perspectives and general wisdom can be effective tools for his mentee's success. Although a mentor and his mentee may talk frequently, the process begins with a delivery of valuable information or insight into the program.

For the program to work well and be a rewarding experience, there are some guidelines that must be met:

- Mentees should be able to rely on their mentors to keep them informed and up-to-date with all important information.

- A mentor should help a mentee develop a plan of action and set goals for success.

- Student-mentees should share their needs and wants and talk to their mentors about what they hope to gain from the program.

- A mentor program is a dynamic system to teach processes, and it requires mutual cooperation between both parties.

- Mentees should be willing to share effective feedback to their mentors, helping them to provide good content.

- A mentor is responsible for developing the mentee's fullest potential and strengths and for eliminating weaknesses that inhibit growth and success.

"Think like a winner and act like a champion, In other words, fake it till you make it!"
Mark Zupo -2009

It should be considered that although you might coach other people in the improvement of their lives, it is even more important that you build trust between you and your mentees.

I charge more than $1,000 per hour with a 3-hour minimum for authoritative mentoring. Mentoring people is one of the most lucrative revenue streams that you will ever find. The process to develop a mentor program is one that can be done anywhere in the world, at any time of the day or week.

-Systemization

The model for mentoring is to mentor many people at one time; although you are selling your knowledge at a cheaper rate because you have delivered the same information to more people at one time as opposed to a few people at one time.

As a mentor, you guide your mentees in the safest and most productive methods or paths that they should take. A clear example of a "mentor" program in the professional world is a franchise. There are many like McDonald's, drug stores, car washes and movie theaters. You can surely understand that a franchise is designed for the franchisees to be as productive and profitable as humanly possible. If the individual store owners succeed and make money, then the company that holds the franchise makes money and everyone is happy.

-Standardization

A huge benefit of a mentorship program is to set up your program so mentees are challenged to perform and to measure their performance. Without measurement and goals, mentees will falter und usually fail, even with your guidance. One of the challenges for someone who owns a franchisee is that he or she cannot alter or wander from the absolute prescribed method, product or practice of the franchise.

-Automation

Contact with your mentees is an

absolute must. Usually you will give them a private method to contact you with questions or problems. Email is one of the best methods to remain in contact to fully understand what the issue is so that the correct response is sent.

-Delegation

A comprehensive program is the best model for your success, as well as for the mentees' success. Pure and concise content, with an all-inclusive program, is the key to making a successful mentor program.

Delegation exists when the mentees have a support partner whose interest in their success is founded on mutual benefit. Once mentees are dedicated to their own success and commit to following your instructions, they will require a complete and comprehensive program to follow.

When you mentor more than one mentee, there is a synergy between mentees and mentor that will have a dynamic life of its own that will benefit everyone who participates.

> *"If you think you can or you think you can't... Either way you're right!"*
>
> — **Henry Ford**

Copy Success

-Get a Mentor, Get a Mentor, and Get a Mentor!

One method that I use to coach people who are reluctant to follow through with an assignment is to require them to sign a check made out for $100 to someone they don't like. Then the check is given to a loyal friend who wants to see them succeed and is sworn to send the check if they fail to perform. The key word here is DON'T like. The thought of giving away your money to someone you don't like is usually a motivator to achievement.

If ever you fail to complete a task assigned, the payment that is pending should scare you back into doing what you should do.

"To find success, you have to begin looking in the right direction, To get to the place where your success lives; you have to start where you stand."

- **Mark Zupo**

A note from Mark

Hello and welcome!

First I would like to say thank you for your trust. I know there is a world of options out there but you chose my book. That is a very humbling and special thing for me.

I am an entrepreneur who has published books, created online home study courses, created digital information books, mentor, trained
and presented at various seminars both in-person and online. For the past 24 years I have been actively involved with mentoring in the success-motivation industry.

As a thought-leader and business mentor I have worked with businesses and people all over the world. I have worked with educators, business owners, individuals, entrepreneurs, lawyers, consultants, coaches, trainers and more. As founder of the ***7-Level Success Academy*®** I have helped these same people achieve personal and business success, improvement to life and happiness. We have helped them increase their customers, increase their sales and increase their profits.

"Make Your Business Your Life and Make Your Life Your Business!"
- **Mark Zupo**

Mind Your Business™

Conclusion

We all understand, regardless of the industry in which we work, that we are in the people business. What differentiates us from the masses is that we understand that we are in the ME business because we have spent an entire lifetime building, educating, improving, detailing, sharpening, motivating, strengthening and training ourselves to be the finest product ever to hit the market. You have improved on the invention of YOU in every way until you have become the tool of choice in your business and industry.

The truest business YOU have ever worked in is the business of your life, and you have never been paid your real value and your real worth. It is time that you be rewarded for a lifetime of labor and attention. The product of YOU is ready and waiting to be unleashed on the world, and now is the time.

The obstacles to success are not the things we think we lack to be successful; the true obstacle is getting rid of the things that we have that get in the way of our success. Successful people do what other people don't want to do.

To Your Success...

Opportunity

Don't Spend Years Trying to Write Your Book!

There is a Fast and Painless Way to Write a Book without Having to Actually Write it Word For Word!

The Secrets to Writing & Selling Your First Book Fast!

The Original How to "Write and Sell Your First Book" Workshop

You have always thought of writing a book, but you just can't find the time, right? Now you can...because I will show you how to do it faster than you ever thought possible!

The **"YourFastBook™"** Workshop will give you all the tools you'll ever need to "blast" out a book in no time flat!

In the "YourFastBook™" workshop, you'll learn:

- ➢ How to write your book without ever putting pen to paper!
- ➢ How to market your book without ever paying a publisher!

- ➢ How to make your book available to millions with a click of a button!
- ➢ How to avoid the 10 most common mistakes authors make!
- ➢ How to protect your copyright with this simple free technique!
- ➢ How never to pay a royalty keeping all the profit for yourself!

Still Not Convinced?

I am the author or co-author of more-than 23 books to date. I am a "best-selling" author and credible authority on the self-publishing secrets that the conventional industry publishers don't want to you to know.

Check this out! When you enroll in my award-winning workshop you'll get all this and more:

- ✓ How to write your book in one day!
- ✓ How to give your book an award-winning title!
- ✓ The three secrets to every author's success with future orders!
- ✓ How to turn your book into a "Money-Machine."
- ✓ How to make people pay five times what you paid for printing!
- ✓ How to develop multiple streams of income from your book.

You MUST get in on this workshop right NOW!

Classes fill up quickly, so <u>sign-up now and become a self-published author</u>!

Workshop Details:

Become an author and wow your friends and relatives. Start your book now by enrolling in this exclusive workshop today!

Follow Mark on Twitter and Facebook for insight, inspiration and motivation with words of wisdom, encouragement and enthusiasm!

Need more proof? See what other authors say about the YourFastBook™ workshop.

"Unbelievable! What could be more fun than writing a book that becomes your signature trademark? I am really proud to be a part of this seminar and see just what anyone could do with the information that they already had. Writing a book is more fun than I ever imagined. I was absolutely amazed at the speed at which I can write a book when I thought that it would take years to complete."

"I could never have imagined that I could be a

published author until I met Mark Zupo. He allowed me to think on a different level about traditional publishing. I am now a self-publishing advocate forever!"

"When I enrolled in Mark's workshop, I was skeptical and reserved to think that I had a book in me that someone would want to read. Now I know that my story is as powerful as any book that has ever been written. I am empowered as a new author to help other people write their story too."

"I've always felt I had a book within me. Years ago, I wanted to be a children's book author. I even took a well-known children's literature course I saw advertised in a magazine, and for which I paid dearly. Rejection slips kept coming back after sending in my queries to traditional publishing companies. I finally said, "To heck with this," and packed all my thoughts and papers away.

"Then, I met Mark. His enthusiasm and down-right sincerity convinced me I could create my own book. Now, I'm a published author! I would not hesitate to tell everyone to take Mark's course. Not only does he know what he's talking about, but he has the proof to back it up."

Are you too far away from Atlanta?

Choose the One-on-One Book eConference Package with Mark Zupo

The Executive Author Conference:

- **eConference 1:** We will nail down the focus of your book, the

title and niche the market wants and needs, and the idea and synopsis. Then we'll devise a plan for writing, printing, marketing and self-publishing it. We will tailor your personal objectives and timeline for completion of the book content. I will give you some of the resources for the writing, printing and publishing you will need at this stage.

- **eConference 2:** Here we will evaluate the content of your book

And formulate questions and the answers that will deliver the information that will become chapters. We'll talk about the process of establishing a brand, finding a market, positioning your book for discovery and creating methods of future income from your book.

- **eConference 3:** In this session we bring together the content, the format and the completeness of the book. We discuss income streams and methods for future books. At this stage we can start to see the results of the book in real life.

Note: We will schedule three one-hour, one-on-one conferences (via Freeconferencecall.com, iChat, Skype or telephone). Also, there will be 2-3 additional hours of discussion via email to unite your work with the industry standard for what a book must contain.
The purpose of this package is to focus your idea and material into a print-ready product to begin your life as a self-published author.

This package is not for people who sit around and talk about how hard it is to write a book! **This package is a proven method of self-publishing.** This is your opportunity to be a self-published author with lightning speed!

SCHEDULE **YOURFASTBOOK™ Executive eConference** now!

A note from Mark

Hello and welcome!

First I would like to say thank you for your trust. I know there is a world of options out there but you chose my book. That is a very humbling and special thing for me.

I am an entrepreneur who has published books, created online home study courses, created digital information books, mentor, trained and presented at various seminars both in-person and online. For the past 24 years I have been actively involved with mentoring in the success-motivation industry.

As a thought-leader and business mentor I have worked with businesses and people all over the world. I have worked with educators, business owners, individuals, entrepreneurs, lawyers, consultants, coaches, trainers and more. As founder of the:
***7 Level Success Academy*®**
 I have helped these same people achieve personal and business success, improvement to life and happiness.

Mark's Books:

1. **"You Deserve to be Rich"**
   The Secrets to Earning What You're Really Worth

2. **From Mess to Millionaire**
   One Man's Story of Failure to Success

3. **Speak for Yourself**
   The 7-Secrets of How to Make your Living Speaking

4. **Dean of the DUMP!**
   What I Learned When I lived at the Garbage Dump!

5. **7Level Success Millionaire**
   Are you born to be RICH?

6. **Write, Publish and Sell Your life Story**
   Turning You Lifelong Experience into Lifelong Income

Appendix One

Sources and Resources

Mark's speaking career in industry spans 25 years. He has delivered more-than, 1,200 presentations. From his experiences he has authored and co-authored many books on self-development, business development techniques and marketing enterprises. Mark speaks on several topics that enlighten, entertain and motivate his audiences to action!

Mark's Most Requested Topics/Programs:
- **My Adversity University**
  "Build Power, Credibility and Respect from Life's Lessons"
- **Champion Your Success**
  "Achieve What You Believe, Believe What You Can Achieve'
- **7-Secrets of Business Success**
  "The Keys to Wealth and Freedom"
- **Leadership**
"From Ability to Credibility"

>Schedule Mark to Speak at Your Next Event!
>Contact us: 1-678-640-0585
>09:00 – 5:00 EST
>On-line:
>www.MarkZupo.com
>markzupo@gmail.com

Questions for Consideration

1. **What has influenced my life in the last 12 months and how can I show appreciation by sharing it?**

   _____

2. **What are my last 5 victories in the past 90 days?**

   _____
   _____
   _____
   _____

3. **What are the 5 things I do very well?**

   _____
   _____
   _____

4. **What are 5 ways I could push out of my comfort zone and what would the payoff be?**

   _____
   _____
   _____

5. **What am I looking forward to in the next 90 days?**

   _____

6. **Who am I and what can I offer?**

16 Questions That Set You Apart

Am I a sponge for discovery and opportunity?
Do I devour information that keeps me sharp to the current events that affect my markets?

Am I a true optimist?
Do I think of problems as opportunities?

Am I forward-looking?
Am I satisfied with the status quo?

Am I a risk-taker?
Do I usually act on my hunches?

Do I have passion?
Do I stick to my efforts instead of quitting? Do I love what I do?

Am I competitive?
Do I think in competitive terms to motivate me?

Am I money wise?
Do I understand costs and values?

Was I an entrepreneur at a young age?
Did I have the entrepreneurial spirit early on?

Am I time conscious?
Do I know the value of time and know how to use it?

Am I overtly curious?
Do I ask a lot of questions about how things work?

Am I a solitary worker?
Do I work best by myself or on a team?

Am I professional at all times?

7-Level Success Seminars™
Mark Zupo Seminars™

...Reserve your seat NOW!

www.7Level Success.com

www.MarkZupo.com

DISCLAIMER

This information in this book is strictly for informational and educational purposes only. The author and/or publisher do not guarantee that anyone using any of the information, tips, techniques, etc. from this book will become successful. The author and/or publisher shall have neither liability nor responsibility to anyone with respect to any loss or damage caused, or alleged to be caused, directly or indirectly by the information contained in this book. No guarantees are made that you will achieve any results from our ideas and techniques in our material. The information presented herein represents the view of the author as of the date of publication. The author reserves the right to alter and update his opinion Any slights of people or organizations are unintentional. You should be aware of any laws which govern business transactions or other business practices in your country and state. Any reference to any person or business whether living or dead is purely coincidental. We do not purport this as a "get rich scheme." All trademarks belong to their respective owners.

The publisher has strived to be as accurate and complete as possible in the creation of this report, notwithstanding the fact that he does not warrant or represent at any time that the contents within are accurate, due to the rapidly changing nature of the business. However, there may be mistakes in typography or content. The purpose of this e-book is to educate.

While all attempts have been made to verify information provided in this publication, the publisher assumes no responsibility for errors, omissions, or contrary interpretation of the subject matter herein. Any perceived slights of specific persons, peoples, or organizations are unintentional.

This book is a common-sense guide to marketing online. In practical advice books, like in anything else in life, there are no guarantees of income made. Readers are cautioned to reply with their own judgment about their individual circumstances and to act accordingly. This book is not intended for use as a source of legal, business, accounting or financial advice. All readers are advised to seek services of competent professionals in legal, business, accounting and finance fields.

This information is presented for educational and informational purposes only and is not intended to be a substitute for professional advice. Never disregard professional advice or delay in seeking it because of something read or heard.

We make every effort to ensure that we accurately represent our products and services and their potential for income. Earning and income statements made by our company and its customers are estimates of what we think you can possibly earn. There is no guarantee that you will make the level of income you desire, and you accept the risk that the earnings and income statements differ by individual.

As with any business, your results may vary and will be based on your individual capacity, business experience, expertise, and level of desire. The testimonials and examples used are exceptional results, which do not apply to the average purchaser, and are not intended to represent or guarantee that anyone will achieve the same or similar results. Each individual's success depends on his or her background, dedication, desire and motivation.

The use of our information, products and services should be based on your own due diligence, and you hold harmless our company for any success or failure of your business that is directly or indirectly related to the purchase and use of our information, products and services.

"Yesterday is history...Tomorrow is a mystery, Today is a gift, which is why it is called the "Present"...

Live for today as though tomorrow never comes!
*-   **Eleanor Roosevelt***

Mind Your Business™

Mark Zupo

Mind Your Business™

Mark Zupo

www.ingramcontent.com/pod-product-compliance
Lightning Source LLC
Chambersburg PA
CBHW071847230426
43671CB00012B/2086